Essentials of Music
For Audio Professionals

A concise course in music fundamentals for engineers, producers, directors, editors, managers, and other audio recording professionals.

By
Frank Dorritie
Chair, Recording Arts Department
Los Medanos College
Pittsburg, California

Edited by Sarah Jones

236 Georgia Street, Suite 100
Vallejo, CA 94590

Library of Congress Catalog Card Number: 00-100264

Art Director: Stephen Ramirez
Cover Design: Linda Gough
Book Design and Layout: Linda Gough
Production Staff: Mike Lawson, publisher; Sarah Jones, editor
Illustrators: Ian Sandiland, Magnus Design
Music Typesetting: Evan Conlee, Con Brio Music

MixBooks is an imprint of artistpro.com, LLC
236 Georgia Street, Suite 100
Vallejo, CA 94590
707-554-1935

Also from MixBooks
The AudioPro Home Recording Course, Volumes I, II and III
I Hate the Man Who Runs this Bar!
How to Make Money Scoring Soundtracks and Jingles
The Art of Mixing: A Visual Guide to Recording, Engineering, and Production
500 Songwriting Ideas (For Brave and Passionate People)
Music Publishing: The Real Road to Music Business Success, Rev. and Exp. 4th Ed.
How to Run a Recording Session
Mix Reference Disc, Deluxe Ed.
The Songwriter's Guide to Collaboration, Rev. and Exp. 2nd Ed.
Critical Listening and Auditory Perception
Modular Digital Multitracks: The Power User's Guide Rev. Ed.
The Dictionary of Music Business Terms
Professional Microphone Techniques
Sound for Picture 2nd Ed.
Music Producers 2nd Ed.
Live Sound Reinforcement

Also from EMBooks:
The Independent Working Musician
Making the Ultimate Demo 2nd Ed.
Making Music with Your Computer 2nd Ed.
Anatomy of a Home Studio
The EM Guide to the Roland VS-880

Printed in Auburn Hills, MI
ISBN 0-87288-737-5

Dedication

To my music mentors. . .

John Sasso
Donald Angelica
Dr. Bernard Baggs
Cal Tjader
and
Art Blakey

. . . for their wisdom and encouragement.

Acknowledgments

I wish to thank the following for their inspiration and support: Shirley Stratton Dorritie, Steve Savage, John Maltester, Nancy Bachmann, Rick Shiner, Dick Livingston, Mike Lawson, Sarah Jones, Richard Greene, Johnny Otis, John Kaizan Neptune, Cam Perry, Patrick Palomo, David Ladd, Geena Jeffries, Franc D'Ambrosio, Phil Edwards, Peter and Gillian Fairhead, Gerry Shellmer, Ralph Hardimon, James Reilly, S.J., Jim Donnelly, Deltra Almeida and the late Carl Jefferson.

—Frank Dorritie

Contents

Preface

There appears to be no shortage of "road maps to the recording studio" written for the musician. This, however, is the first book (to my knowledge) to address the musical needs of producers, engineers and others whose training and experience are in the technical (rather than musical) arts.

My experiences in hundreds of recording sessions have taught me the immeasurable value of working with engineers who have a strong fundamental grounding in music. These individuals, comfortable in both musical and technical languages, enhance the session. This combination of skills creates opportunities for them to work more often and at a higher level than their sisters and brothers who, though familiar with decibels and hertz, don't know a sostenuto from a stage box.

I searched for a book like this for my audio engineering and video production students. Finding none, I wrote this one. Data was collected from industry publications, college syllabi, standard texts, audio and video recordings, as well as personal experience in the recording studio, classroom, rehearsal hall, and live performance.

My mentors, colleagues, and students supplied the information herein. The responsibility for any errors or misjudgments is mine.

How To Use This Book

This volume is designed for use as reference, text, and workbook. Individual topic headings have not been prioritized, since each is important to a grasp of the subject at an introductory level. Nor do these particular concepts collectively provide an exhaustive survey, only a starting point.

The sequence of presentation, though flexible according to the reader's needs, is arranged to form a logical, if unorthodox, progression. The glossary contains terms most often encountered in college-level basic music courses, and additional references useful to recording professionals. Musical concepts are presented in greater detail under the chapter headings. Also, many concepts are supplemented with recorded examples, which can be found on the accompanying audio CD; practical exercises for skills enhancement appear when appropriate.

There are numerous learning styles, which will dictate a variety of approaches to the use of this book. It is recommended, however, that the book be perused once "cover to cover" before in-depth study begins. This overview will prove beneficial to virtually any reader.

Understanding Music...

"...sounds pleasing to the ear, either in
succession or in combination."
—John Philip Sousa

"...rhythm, pitch, and expression."
—John Sasso

"One may know how to read printed books,
yet not know how to read the unprinted ones;
be able to play on a stringed harp, yet not on a
stringless one. Studying the superficial instead
of the profound, how will one understand music
or poetry?"
—Zen saying

CHAPTER 1

Audio Sample Log

AUDIO SAMPLE   TITLE

1....Mogamigawa Funa Uta
2....Poppin' the Rag
3....Quarter Notes
4....Eighth Notes
5....Sixteenth Notes
6....Rembetiko
7....Brentwood Rag
8....Obey Me
9....Mozart
10....Tarantella
11....Mambo Jalambo
12....Chimes
13....Mozart
14....Row, Row, Row Your Boat
15....Pop Goes the Weasel
16....Goin' Home
17....Hatikvah
18....Belize
19....Minuet
20....First Concerto for Guitar and Orchestra
21....Jupiter
22....Panis Angelicus
23....C-Major Scale
24....C-Minor Scale
25....C Harmonic Minor
26....C Melodic Minor—Ascending/Descending
27....Relative Minor
28....Whole Tone Scale
29....Blues Scale
30....Pentatonic Scale
31....F-Sharp Pentatonic Scale
32....Japanese Scale
33....Chinese Scale
34....Azerbaijani Scale
35....Ugandan Scale
36....Indian Scale

Music As Concept

CULTURAL CONTEXT

Music is frequently referred to as a kind of language. It might be more instructive to think of language as a kind of music, and music as purposeful sound, plain and simple. However it is defined, music is ubiquitous and transcultural; and therefore, indispensable to the understanding of the universe. Narrowing the focus slightly, a solid understanding of music's fundamentals will enhance both the artistic experience itself and one's career prospects in the industry.

The earliest music was probably oral, in imitation of the sounds of nature. It was also aural, in the sense that it was learned by ear and stored only in the memory. As late as the 7th century in Europe, rhythm and pitch could not be precisely represented in a visual system, only indicated generally. Indeed, today's systems of quantizing and symbolizing the musical idea, though fairly standardized, remain incomplete. Storing music in visual form for later retrieval is convenient but depersonalized. Accessing it in audio form is enjoyable, but essentially passive. To understand music, it is necessary to think of it as experiential in essence, oral and aural.

The term "music" is derived from the Greek *muses,* mythological personifications of artistic inspiration. In Indian tradition, the God *Siva,* having created music and dance, taught them to his consort, *Sri,* who began the process of passing them on to all creatures. (Interestingly, the animals received them before humans.) The ancient Chinese believed that an early emperor, *HuangTi,* directed bamboo pipes to be cut and given to the astrologers so that vibrations could be matched to the frequencies of the male and female forces of the universe, *Yin* and *Yang.* Nigerian legend holds that *Orgardie,* an Ibuzo hunter, learned music and dance by eavesdropping on forest spirits. An ancient Japanese story credits the female deity *Ame no Uzume* with creating music to entice the return of the Sun Goddess. Holy ones who travel on sun beams bring music to the people, according to the Navajo legend.

Clearly, most of the world holds music in high cultural esteem, even as a spiritual experience. And for most of history music was passed along personally, by example and demonstration, complete with obvious expression and subtle nuance, from one generation to the next, through oral/aural transmission. In this book, the term "oral" will encompass both ideas.

ORAL TRADITION: RECALLING AND RELATING THE EVENT

Important traditions, though ancient in origin, continue to manifest themselves. The oral tradition lives in any music learned exclusively or even partially by ear; nursery songs, national anthems, limericks, rap, blues, rock, even opera. (Luciano Pavarotti, one of the finest opera tenors of all time, learns all his music by rote, from recordings and vocal coaches.) A great deal of music is passed on by learning through listening and repeating.

AUDIO SAMPLE 1

"Mogamigawa Funa Uta (Mogami River Boat Song)" (trad.)
(Kaizan Music/ASCAP) John Kaizan Neptune, Shakuhachi.
From *Words Can't Go There* (Oasis Productions NHCD 204)

The oral tradition is a common thread, and indeed the foundation of, all musical forms. The idea of musical accompaniment to storytelling is universal and ongoing. A culture's identity is revealed in its art: Attitudes toward self, others, and the universe are defined and clarified through musical storytelling, also known as popular song. Recalling or relating an event, embellishing heroic deeds and reputations, advertising for a mate, displaying universal emotions, and identifying with the life of the common person—these acts and more have been orally nurtured throughout human history, from the epic *Vedic* stories of India, to Homer, to hip hop.

NOTATION: VISUALIZING THE MUSICAL EVENT

Why develop a symbolic written form for music? Most importantly, as a memory aid, a guide. Cave paintings reveal humankind's wish to not only decorate life with reminders of truth, but to pass those truths generationally, to store them for the future. The Greeks had a system for writing music by the 6th century, consisting of neumes, symbols indicating general pitch direction for chant. Some 400 years later, these symbols began to appear along with a single horizontal line, which represented a reference pitch. Around 1200, in Germany, square symbols were appearing on a four-line staff system, defining actual pitches. Eventually, much of Europe developed the five-line, four-space staff in current use.

Whereas oral transmission requires a meeting between teacher and student, written music notation allows transfer of musical information without demonstration. Clearly, a written system enhanced the worldwide dissemination of European musical culture.

Musical forms were originally memory aids. Systems for writing music encouraged more complexity and de-emphasized the importance of memorizing. Notation promoted consistency and standardization, and restricted the interpretive and improvisational freedoms of the performer. Written music made large ensembles viable, and gave the composer expanded possibilities for creating textures and effects previously unavailable. Composers took creative advantage of the medium to develop new and extended forms (opera, symphony, concerto), but melody persisted as the elemental unit.

RECORDING: DOCUMENTING THE EVENT

Consider this: One can purchase a booklet of the songs popularized by Bob Dylan. Since much of the essential information about form and content is printed in symbolic form, a person with a modest amount of musical training can learn all of the tunes well enough to perform them. Or, one can acquire a Bob Dylan CD anthology (or, better, a video of concert performances). Ironically, the recording media—visual and audio—constitute a further development in the oral tradition; the next best thing to having witnessed the performance in person. Recorded documents (audio, video, and printed) have the advantage of permitting virtually unlimited review and study of the captured event. Still, without experiencing live performance (as listener or participant) there will be critical gaps in understanding music. The professional takes advantage of all sources of information.

Essentials of Music for Audio/Video Professionals

Rhythmic Notation

The closest ancestor of modern rhythmic notation was a system of square neumes that came into use in Germany in the 13th century. This system is called mensural notation.

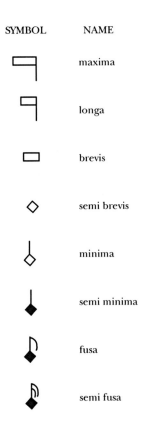

SYMBOL	NAME
	maxima
	longa
	brevis
	semi brevis
	minima
	semi minima
	fusa
	semi fusa

Like all note values, these are relative rather than absolute. From top to bottom, each note has fifty percent of the duration of its predecessor. These forms evolved into current standard notation:

SYMBOL	AMERICAN SYSTEM	BRITISH SYSTEM
𝅝	whole note	semibreve
𝅗𝅥	half note	minim
𝅘𝅥	quarter note	crotchet
𝅘𝅥𝅮	eighth note	quaver
𝅘𝅥𝅯	sixteenth note	semiquaver
𝅘𝅥𝅰	thirty-second note	demisemiquaver
𝅘𝅥𝅱	sixty-fourth note	hemidemisemiquaver

Here, again, each note represents fifty percent of the relative duration value of its predecessor. Note values have corresponding rests, indicating periods of silence:

SYMBOL	NAME
▬	whole rest
▬	half rest
𝄽	quarter rest
𝄾	eighth rest
𝄿	sixteenth rest
𝅀	thirty-second rest
𝅁	sixty-fourth rest

The same relative values apply: Top to bottom, each rest has fifty percent of the duration value of the one above. If a dot is added to a note or a rest, the duration of the composite increases by fifty percent:

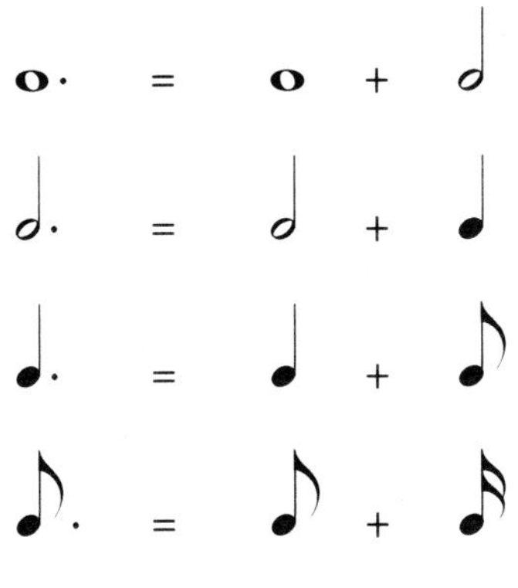

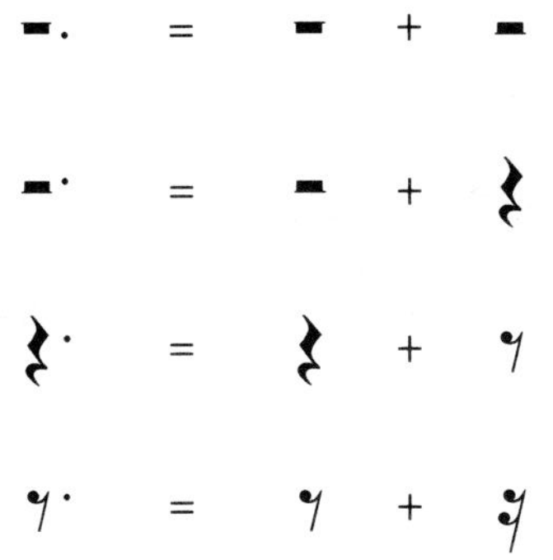

𝅝. = 𝅝 + 𝅗𝅥

𝅗𝅥. = 𝅗𝅥 + 𝅘𝅥

𝅘𝅥. = 𝅘𝅥 + 𝅘𝅥𝅮

𝅘𝅥𝅮. = 𝅘𝅥𝅮 + 𝅘𝅥𝅯

𝄻. = 𝄻 + 𝄼

𝄼. = 𝄼 + 𝄽

𝄽. = 𝄽 + 𝄾

𝄾. = 𝄾 + 𝄿

Note values are sometimes connected by ties. Both notes are then played as one, without separation, with their values added together:

𝅗𝅥‿𝅘𝅥 = 𝅗𝅥 + 𝅘𝅥 = 𝅘𝅥.

COMPONENTS OF THE NOTE

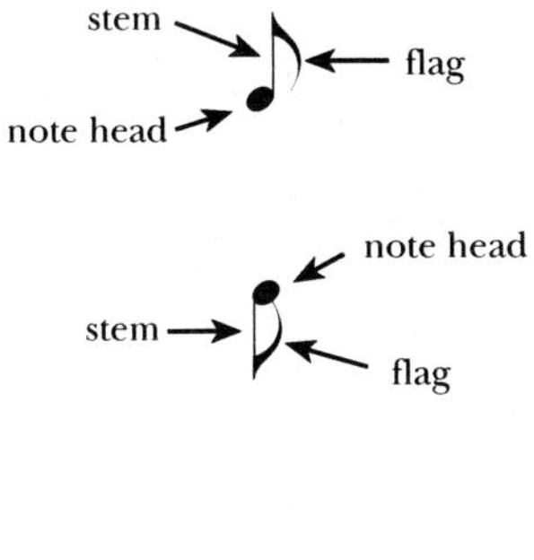

stem → ↘ 𝅘𝅥𝅮 ← flag

note head →

note head ↖

stem → ← flag

RELATIVE NOTE VALUES

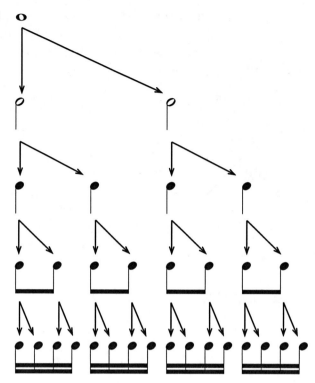

RELATIVE REST VALUES

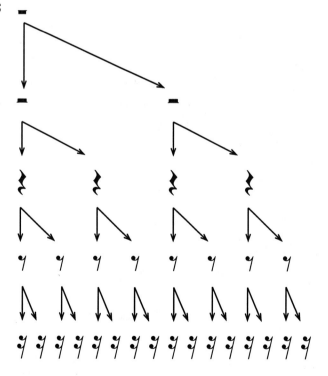

Rhythm is a specific pattern of beats. The concept of division by two is natural to human beings. Physically, we are essentially symmetrical, with two eyes, ears, nostrils, lungs, arms, legs, feet, etc. Counting in multiples of two, then, should be a recognizable behavior pattern. Consider walking:

left, right, left, right, etc.
Or swimming:
stroke, stroke, stroke, stroke/turn head and breathe, etc.
(Kicking the feet four times with each stroke further subdivides into two.)

These are movements humans perform naturally and/or learn easily. The intellectual (and certainly physical) stretch to comprehend rhythmic subdivisions and their symbols is eminently achievable. The walking rhythm above can be represented, visually as follows:

(These symbols could also represent hands or sticks striking drum heads.)

These notes could be considered bits in a numerical code. For convenience in visual scanning, these individual bits (beats) of information can be grouped, like bytes, with the musical symbol called the bar line, creating measures.

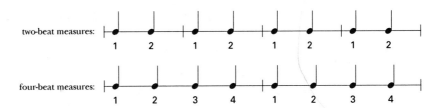

Variations on this most basic of rhythms can be achieved by substituting note combinations for any of the given quarter notes:

This rhythm should be familiar to anyone who has watched a cheerleading performance:

Sometimes in music, the rhythm appears alone, via drums or hand claps. In a rhythmic phrase, the second measure is often antiphonal; that is, an answer to the first. A familiar "door knock" rhythm can be written this way:

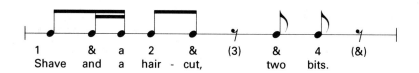

Or, alternately:

The symbol ¢, for alla breve or "cut time," indicates playing the note durations as if they had fifty percent of the value shown. In both cases, the rhythm is identical; context would determine selection.

Ironically, the cultural messengers who brought this rhythm from Africa to the West Indies to New Orleans to rock music (the "Bo-Diddley" rhythm) never represented it visually. It was part of their oral tradition, just as it is part of yours. You and the cheerleaders are well acquainted with these beat patterns, although you may not have visualized them until now. You are reading rhythms. Reading music.

A common variation of this rhythm is accomplished by replacing some of the notes with rests (durations of silence):

Another method for achieving much the same effect is to express accents (>) on some of the notes, thereby de-emphasizing others: (Note: In Latin music, this rhythm is referred to as the forward clave pattern.)

VISUALIZING A FAMILIAR RHYTHM
....

*Listen to **AUDIO SAMPLE 2** several times while reading this rhythm. Repeat the process until you can clap or tap in time with the tape. There is no need to memorize this rhythm; you've already done that. The idea is to mentally and physically reinforce the connections among sound, sensation, and symbol. Follow this procedure whenever written examples of audio samples are provided.*

AUDIO SAMPLE 2

"Poppin' The Rag" (excerpt) (Otis, Parry, Dorritie) Johnny Otis and the Mighty Prince Singers. From *You Made Me Love You* soundtrack (Soaring Dove Productions)

CLAPPING QUARTER NOTES
....

The following group of rhythmic exercises is based on quarter notes and rests at 90 beats per minute. They are grouped in four-beat units (measures) within a phrase of eight measures. Two measures of rest separate each phrase. Listen to the recording while reading the phrases, then repeat several times, clapping or tapping while reading. (You may find it quite helpful to alternately tap your feet, as if walking.) Repeat until you can perform the entire sequence of exercises without error.

Essentials of Music for Audio Professionals

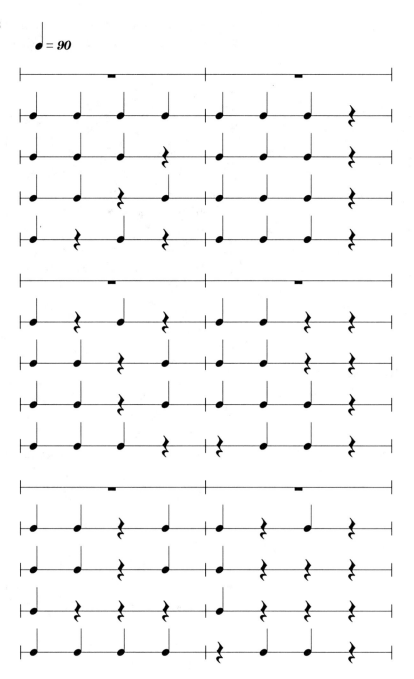

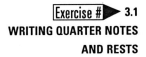
Refer to the previous page and construct three clapping exercises, consisting of eight measures of four beats each, using quarter notes and rests.

|————————————|————————————|

|————————————|————————————|

|————————————|————————————|

|————————————|————————————|

|————————————|————————————|

|————————————|————————————|

|————————————|————————————|

|————————————|————————————|

|————————————|————————————|

|————————————|————————————|

|————————————|————————————|

|————————————|————————————|

Clap or tap these rhythms while reading along, until the entire sequence can be performed without error.

In most music notation, the quarter note is the most common unit of counting—that is, it represents a single beat. (Technically, it is one quarter of a whole note.)

A single beat can be subdivided into two components, the down beat and the up beat. Consider the "walking" rhythm consisting of continuous quarter notes at ♩= *120* (120 quarter notes per minute):

If each quarter note beat is subdivided into two eighth notes, the groupings can be counted as follows:

The sequential (counting) numbers are vocalizations of the down-beat, the "&'s" represent the up-beats. Any rhythm pattern containing eighth notes can be conceptualized and vocalized in this manner, for example:

Or

Clap and vocalize the following patterns, reading along while listening to **AUDIO SAMPLE 4**. *Repeat until sequence can be performed without error.*

Essentials of Music for Audio Professionals

Exercise # ▶ **3.2**

**WRITING EIGHTH NOTES
AND RESTS**

*Refer to the previous examples and construct three clapping/vocalizing
exercises, consisting of eight measures of four beats each, using quarter
notes, eighth notes, and their corresponding rests (durations of silence).*

*Clap these rhythms, while vocalizing and reading along, until the entire
sequence can be performed without error.*

If each eighth note is subdivided into two sixteenths, the groupings can be counted as follows:

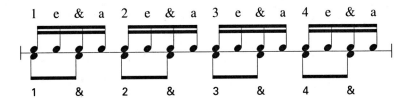

Note that the counting numbers (one, two, etc.) remain on the down beats while the "ands" remain on the up beats.

Verbalize the following pattern, keeping a consistent tempo (speed) and reading the note symbols:

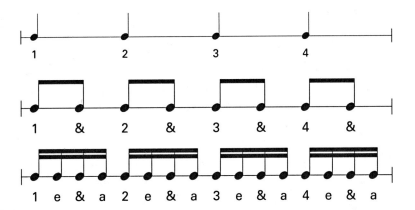

*Clap and vocalize the following patterns, reading along, while listening to **AUDIO SAMPLE 5**.*

AUDIO SAMPLE 5

♩ = *60*

Repeat until sequence can be performed without error.

Exercise # ▶ **3.3**

**WRITING SIXTEENTH
NOTES AND RESTS**

*Construct three clapping/vocalizing exercises, consisting of eight
measures of four beats each, using eighth notes, sixteenth notes, and
their corresponding rests.*

*Clap these rhythms, while vocalizing and reading along, until the entire
sequence can be performed without error.*

TIME SIGNATURE/METER

These symbols were developed to indicate the general metrical
pattern of a musical piece. The time signature is expressed as a
kind of fraction, without the horizontal line.

The top number indicates how many beats in each
measure. The bottom number indicates which note symbol
counts as one beat.

Essentials of Music for Audio Professionals

TWO-FOUR TIME: 2—number of beats per measure

4—quarter note is one beat

Therefore, in a two-four composition, each measure will contain two beats, each beat being a quarter note (or its equivalent). Here is a common polka rhythm pattern:

FOUR-FOUR TIME: 4—number of beats per measure

4—quarter note is one beat

This is such a common meter that it is referred to as common time. (All the rhythm exercises to this point in Chapter 3 have been in four-four time).

Note: The terms meter and time signature are used interchangeably and are independent of tempo, which indicates speed, rather than pattern. (In musical slang, however, someone who "has good time" possesses accurate metrical feel as well as the ability to hold tempo.)

METRIC CLASSIFICATIONS

In European music there are three types of meter: simple, compound, and asymmetrical.

1) SIMPLE METERS—Each beat in a measure of simple meter is divisible by two; that is, the metric unit can be divided into two of the next smaller note values. Meters are further classified into duple, triple, and quadruple.

SIMPLE DUPLE	SIMPLE TRIPLE	SIMPLE QUADRUPLE
2	3	4
2	2	2
2	3	4
4	4	4
2	3	4
8	8	8

2) COMPOUND METERS—Each beat of a compound meter is divisible by three; that is, the metric unit can be divided into three of the next smaller note values.

COMPOUND DUPLE

Compound Duple

Two dotted half notes can be divided into three quarter notes each:

Two dotted quarter notes = three eighth notes each:

COMPOUND TRIPLE

Compound Triple

Three dotted half notes = three quarter notes each:

Three dotted quarter notes = three eighth notes each:

COMPOUND QUADRUPLE

Compound Quadruple

Four dotted half notes = three quarter notes each:

Four dotted quarter notes = three eighth notes each:

These are the basic note groupings and represent the usual divisions of the measures. Other groupings are often encountered, but all note values within the measure must match these equivalents when summed. For example:

three groups of
two eighth notes

one group of
three eighth notes

This pattern changes the rhythmic pulse but not the meter, since there are still nine eighth notes, or their metric equivalent, in each bar. (This example shows the pattern of Dave Brubeck's "Blue Rondo a la Turk.")

3) ASYMMETRICAL METERS—These are the result of combining dissimilar simple meters.

ASYMMETRICAL METERS

5	combination of: 3	and	2
4	4		4
5	combination of: 3	and	2
8	8		8
7	combination of: 4	and	3
4	4		4
7	combination of: 4	and	3
8	8		8

Music is sometimes written in alternating meters.
For example:

(This is the meter of "America" from *West Side Story*, written by Leonard Bernstein and Stephen Sondheim.)

$\frac{4}{4}$ or **C**   Four-Four Time, or Common Time

The top number indicates that there are four beats per measure, the bottom that the quarter note gets one beat. (It is the metric unit.) This is by far the most frequently encountered meter, especially so in pop, rock, jazz, blues, and folk music. Each time signature has its own pattern of implied accents (pulses); the four-four pulse pattern is:

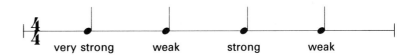

In four-four time, the down-beat of one is the strongest pulse in the measure, beat three is less strong, beats two and four are weak. For example:

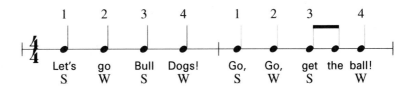

AUDIO SAMPLE 6

"**Rembetiko**" (Otis, Parry, Dorritie), from *You Made Me Love You* soundtrack (Soaring Dove Productions)

This rembetiko is a type of Greek folk song with a tango-like feel. It is a clear example of the underlying pulse pattern in four-four time. Listen for this pattern throughout:

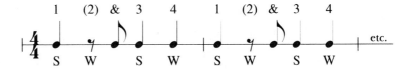

Two-Two Time, or Cut Time

In this meter, there are two beats per measure and the metric unit is the half note. In two-two time, the down-beat of one is the strong pulse. For example:

Notice that two-two ("cut time") looks identical to four-four. In fact, it is written and read like common time, but played twice as fast. Cut time is frequently used to represent complex rhythms, since it simplifies the notation. This is especially common in jazz and Latin music.

AUDIO SAMPLE 7

"Brentwood Rag" (Dorritie), Soaring Dove Productions. Tom McManus, piano.

Although this example can be counted in a fast four, it is written in cut-time for convenience.

"Waltz Time"

In this meter there are three beats per measure and the metric unit is the quarter note. Not every piece in three-four time is a waltz, but that dance achieved such popularity that it became virtually synonymous with the meter.

In three-four time, beat **one** is the strong pulse, **two** and **three** are weak. For example:

AUDIO SAMPLE 8

"Obey Me" (Otis, Parry, Dorritie), from *You Made Me Love You* soundtrack (Soaring Dove Productions). Tom McManus, piano.

Two-Four Time

In this meter there are two beats per measure and the metric unit is the quarter note. Beat **one** is the strong pulse.

AUDIO SAMPLE 9

Turkish March (Mozart). David Ladd, flute.

This example of two-four features a two-note "pick-up" (anacrusis) to beat one of the first measure.

 Six-Eight Time

In this meter there are six beats per measure, divided into two groups of three eighth notes. Beats **one** and **four** are the strong pulses. Six-eight time is quite a common meter for folk dances, classical music, marches, and pop ballads. Although it is based on the eighth note, the metric unit is generally considered to be the dotted quarter (♩.), the equivalent of three eighths. For example:

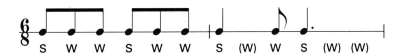

AUDIO SAMPLE 10

"Tarantella" (Otis, Parry, Dorritie), from *You Made Me Love You* soundtrack (Soaring Dove Productions)

This piece is based on a traditional Italian folk dance, the tarantella, which was believed to cure the poisonous bite of the spider.

 Twelve-Eight Time, or "Shuffle"

The true swing feel in jazz and blues, like much other oral music, can only be approximated in written form. Twelve-eight is one of those approximations. The metric unit is the dotted quarter note, four to a bar. The Beach Boys' "California Girls" has a strong shuffle feel.

Essentials of Music for Audio Professionals

(Groupings and strong pulses vary)

5   five beats per measure
4   quarter note is metric unit

6   six beats per measure
4   dotted half note is metric unit

7   seven beats per measure
4   quarter note is metric unit

7   seven beats per measure
8   eighth note is metric unit

9   nine beats per measure
8   dotted quarter note (three eighths) is metric unit

Other meters exist based on half, quarter, eighth, and even sixteenth notes, especially in non-European (Western) music. Often music in these time signatures is learned by rote; that is, by repetition and memorization. Understand that there is a great deal of music that pre-dates any system for writing it and subsequent attempts to quantify it or render it symbolically are, at best, only approximations.

TYPES OF RHYTHM

Meter is the general metrical pattern of a piece as indicated by the time signature. Rhythm is a specific pattern formed by a sequence of note values. Rhythms are divided into four types:

1) UNIFORM—Note values are uniformly distributed in a one-to-one relationship with beats in the measure:

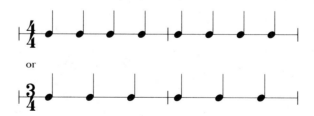

2) REGULAR—Longer note values fall on the strong pulses:

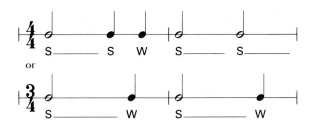

3) IRREGULAR—Shorter note values fall on the strong pulses:

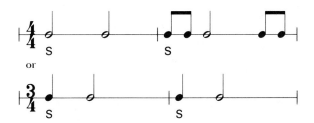

4) SYNCOPATED—A temporary shift of accent to a normally weak beat or between beats.

In a broader sense, the term syncopation indicates any variation in the normal or underlying rhythm of a piece. Listen for unexpected accents in the example.

AUDIO SAMPLE 11

"Mambo Jalambo" (Palomo) Patrick Palomo. From *Piti Village* (Monarch Records MR 1002)

Artificial groupings are clusters of evenly spaced notes, designated by a bracket ⌐, played in the metrical space of a smaller group. Consider quarter notes in common time:

Subdivide to eighth notes:

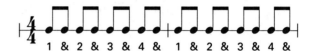

The result is two evenly spaced notes across one beat. To notate three evenly spaced notes across one beat, the triplet is used:

Consider the rhythm of the following:

I like all pies,
cherry pie and apple pie
blueberry, strawberry, all kinds of pies.

The rhythm of the words could be notated thus:

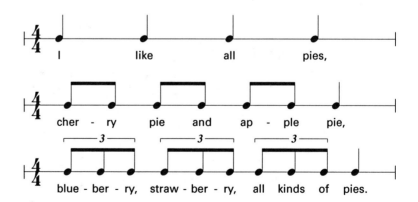

The eighth-note triplet indicates three equal notes on the beat, a space normally subdivided into two eighth notes (or their equivalent). Likewise, the quarter-note triplet fits the space usually occupied by two quarter notes (or their equivalent).

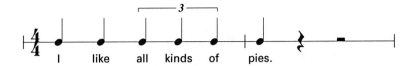

I   like   all   kinds   of   pies.

Triplets are the most common of the artificial groupings. The sixteenth-note triplet appears in such diverse contexts as Celtic folk music and hip hop. This hip hop dance rhythm is built on sixteenth note triplets. The kick drum part is highly syncopated; i.e., normally weak beats are strongly accented:

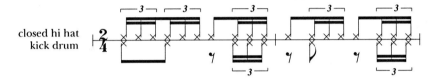

closed hi hat
kick drum

(Noteheads for drum parts are often represented this way, indicating indefinite pitch.)

COMMON RHYTHM UNITS

Examples of using the quarter note as the metric unit:

ONE BEAT

TWO BEATS

Exercise # ▶ 3.4
DIVIDING INTO MEASURES

Divide the following into measures, as dictated by the time signatures. Each example begins on the downbeat of "one." (Answers are in Chapter 13.)

REPEAT SYMBOLS

1) DOUBLE BAR WITH TWO DOTS

Play to here, then repeat from here.

Repeat everything between the two sets of dots, then go on. (If there are no forward-facing dots, repeat from the beginning.)

2) FIRST AND SECOND ENDINGS

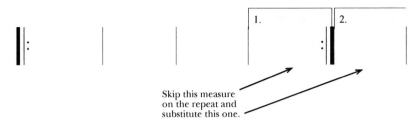

Skip this measure on the repeat and substitute this one.

On repeat, skip [1. and substitute [2.

3) D.C. (DA CAPO)—Repeat from the beginning.

4) D.S. (DAL SEGNO)—Repeat from the sign 𝄋 to the end (fine).

THE FERMATA

𝄐 The fermata indicates holding the note or rest for an indefinite period, determined by the player or conductor.

Pitch Notation

Pitch can be described as the frequency of a sound, expressed in music as a note. Notes are represented by the letter names A-G. The staff, or stave, is a graph that indicates (among other music components) relative pitch. A staff contains five horizontal lines and four spaces, upon which notes are placed.

THE GREAT STAFF

The great or grand staff is actually two staves, one in the bass register and one in the treble, separated by middle *C*:

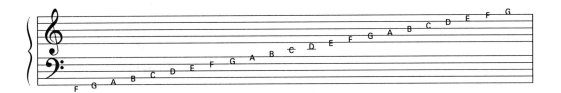

Note that degrees of the staff, lines and spaces, are assigned letter names.

Clefs are symbols added to the staff to define absolute pitch values. The treble clef, 𝄞, marks the location of G (the clef curls around the *G*-line) in the upper staff, and is also known as the *G* clef. The bass clef, 𝄢, indicates the location of *F* (between the clef's two dots) in the lower staff, and is also known as the *F* clef. These symbols are, in fact, idealized versions of those two letters.

Obviously, there are musical pitches that extend beyond the upper and lower limits of the great staff. To accommodate some of these, leger (or ledger) lines, short horizontal lines representing extensions of the staff, are added.

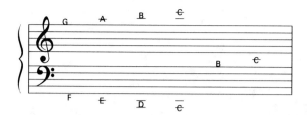

Sounding ranges of many instruments extend beyond these added lines as well; so for convenience in reading, music for these voices is often written an octave above or below where it actually sounds, placing the notes on or near the staff.

While the *F* and *G* clefs remain fixed in their positions on the staff, there is also a movable clef, now rarely used except for cello, viola and (less often) trombone and french horn—instruments whose ranges mostly fall between the treble and bass clefs. It has various names:

C CLEF
SOPRANO CLEF
MEZZO SOPRANO CLEF
ALTO CLEF
TENOR CLEF

The *C* clef is used to designate middle *C* (where the curls meet) at various positions so that music for these voices, which actually sound between the standard staves or above them, can be written without the constant use of ledger lines.

LOCATION OF MIDDLE C

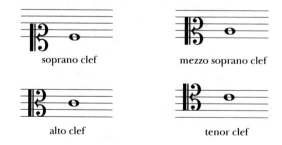

soprano clef   mezzo soprano clef

alto clef   tenor clef

This movable *C* clef will occasionally be encountered in orchestral, opera, and choral scores.

In music, identifying pitches by letter name is more convenient than using numerical frequencies. Scientific instruments that measure these with precision are a relatively recent development and the general agreement designating the *a* above middle *c* at 440 Hz is even more recent. The following letter system is used to differentiate octaves (intervals between a pitch and one double its frequency), subdivided into scale degrees:

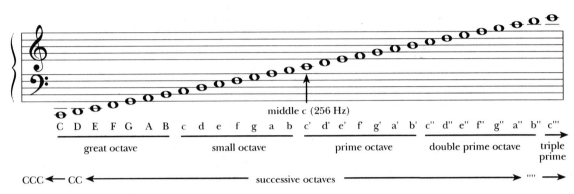

NOTE: Each octave here begins on a *"C"*

VISUAL PITCH IDENTIFICATION

Visual pitch identification is a matter of observation, repetition, and familiarization. Notice, for instance, that a letter-named pitch may be located on a line or in a space, depending on the octave in which it appears. The following exercise will be beneficial.

Identify the pitch by letter name and octave, using the preceding letter code:

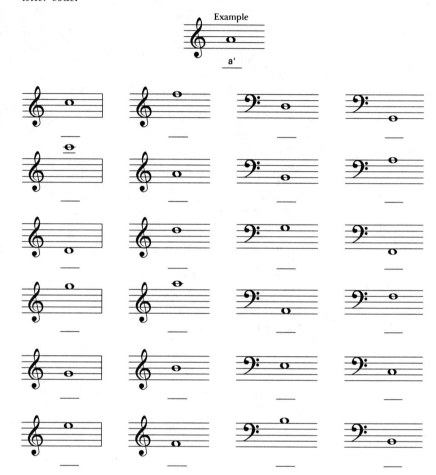

The modern piano, with its seven octaves, has an approximate frequency range of 27 Hz to 4.1 kHz, encompassing the ranges of virtually all other instruments and voices. Consequently, it is a valuable tool for visualizing relationships among voices—basic familiarity with the keyboard is essential.

Study the following templates carefully and refer to them often. They reveal an enormous amount of data vital to the audio/video professional, and will clarify many issues which will follow in this text.

Access to a keyboard will enhance and accelerate the learning process for musical concepts.

OCTAVE TEMPLATE

NOTE: On a piano, *C* is the white key located immediately to the left of the two black keys.

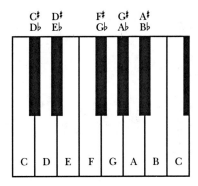

The black keys identify sharps and flats, also known as accidentals (see chapter 10).

The following chart displays notes on the grand staff, with their corresponding frequencies, letter names, and location on the piano keyboard. Also shown are the relative pitch ranges of various voices and string and wind instruments.

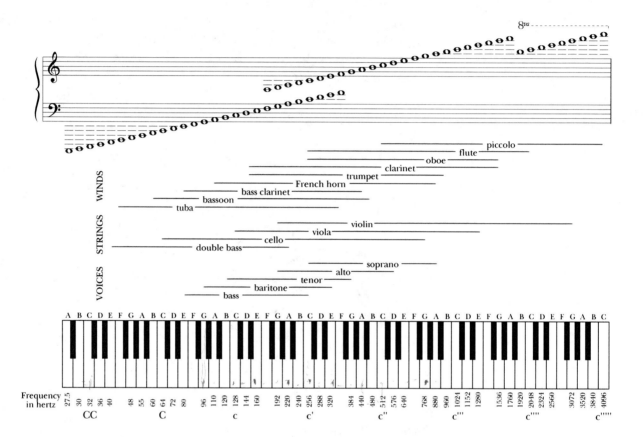

Referring to the template, locate the following pitches on the staff and list their frequencies. Use whole notes.

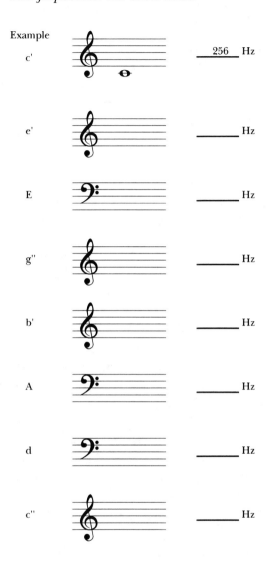

Example

c'   256 Hz

e'   _____ Hz

E   _____ Hz

g"   _____ Hz

b'   _____ Hz

A   _____ Hz

d   _____ Hz

c"   _____ Hz

Musical Expression

Expression is the human element in music. Unlike rhythm and pitch, it cannot be quantified, only suggested. Perfect pitch and rhythmic precision, alone or in combination, do not constitute music any more than the pre-recorded voice of the directory assistance operator constitutes conversation, or the interactive video game constitutes social contact.

Quantizing expression is hopeless. Written music is replete with expression marks indicating directions for performing nuances and embellishments. Performers spend countless hours "perfecting" these musical devices, striving for consistency and uniformity; yet expression is not technique, however refined and polished.

Mastery of these "techniques" will, of course, enhance the performer's ability to be expressive with the music in much the same way that a good vocabulary allows one to express nuance of meaning conversationally. But the the meaning, the feeling, comes first. The notation symbols are nothing more than an attempt to signify something that expressive musicians have been doing since ancient time; that is, bringing their points of view to the music. Expression marks are the composer's attempt to impose a point of view—nothing more, nothing less.

The amount of latitude the individual player has is inversely proportionate to the number of performers. The soloist has the most license to bend the pitch, stretch or compress the tempo, and vary intensity levels, articulations, ornaments or embellishments. Still, it is the composer's vision that is suggested by written expression marks. It will be helpful to bear that in mind. After all, the written music can only tell the performer how long, how loud, how high…expression is not a function of ink, but of humanity.

Changing dynamic level over time is the most common expression technique. It implies a change in proximity of the sound source. (Bringing up an instrument's level in a mix can have a similar effect.) An increase in loudness level signals approach. Things that are closer, more imminent, are, by implication, more urgent and important than background data. (Another recording analogy is close-miking an instrument.) A decrease in level implies withdrawal, resolution, repose, or perhaps anticipation of a sound event to follow. Below is a list of terms indicating changes in dynamic level over time.

SYMBOL	TRANSLATION
<	*crescendo (cresc.)*—a gradual increase in loudness.
>	*decrescendo/diminuendo (decresc./dim.)*—a gradual reduction in loudness.
<>	*crescendo-decrescendo (cresc.-decresc.)*—an increase in loudness followed by a decrease.
p	*piano*—soft (immediately).
pp	*pianissimo*—very soft (immediately).
ppp	*pianississimo*—extremely soft (immediately).
f	*forte*—loud (immediately).
ff	*fortissimo*—very loud (immediately).
fff	*fortississimo*—extremely loud (immediately).
mp	*mezzo-piano*—moderately soft.
mf	*mezzo-forte*—moderately loud.
>	*rinforzando (rfz)*—sudden accent.
sfz	*sforzando*—sudden forceful accent.
–	*tenuto*—note sustained for full value and accented.
–	*martellato*—"hammered" with both hands (piano), short and firm (violin).
Ped.	*pedal*—use damper pedal on piano.
Λ	*marcato*—accent the attack.

Technically, the last six are considered articulations, but they also result in changes in dynamic level, albeit transient ones.

Tempo, the speed at which music is performed, is selected to convey a mood or feeling. Interpretation of tempo instructions is largely subjective; the following is a list of terms defining relative tempo and tempo changes.

TERM	TRANSLATION
accelerando (abbr. accel.)	growing steadily faster.
stringendo (abbr. string.)	quickening.
veloce	faster than before.
velocissimo	as fast as possible.
allargando	gradually slower, with crescendo.
rallentando (abbr. rall.)	gradually slower, no decrescendo.
ritardando (abbr. rit., ritard.)	gradually slower.
ritenuto (abbr. rit.)	slower, held back.

A large aspect of musical expression is articulation, which gives definiton and shape to note and phrase values. The following page lists terms and symbols indicating directions for articulation.

Essentials of Music for Audio Professionals

SYMBOL   TRANSLATION

staccato (stac.)—play shortened notes, emphasize the space.

fermata—pause; hold note, extend duration.

legato (leg.)—lengthen note duration to connect the notes of the phrase smoothly.

slur—play these two notes seamlessly, usually without articulating connecting notes.

breath mark—breathe here (winds).

up bow—(string bowing instruction)

down bow—(string bowing instruction)

trill—slur rapidly between note indicated and next higher note.

acciaccatura—(with slash) a grace note played before the principal note and not counted in the value of the measure.

appoggiatura—(without slash) An embellishment note played with emphasis on the beat.

bend—flatten the note, then return to true pitch.

scoop—begin the note under true pitch and rise to pitch center.

glissando—slide from one note to another rapidly, paying all posible pitches in between.

shake—a wide trill effect produced on horns by shaking the instrument while rapidly changing embouchure (mouth position).

mordent—embellish the principal note with neighboring grace notes.
(inverted)
(double)

doit—play the note on pitch, then slur upward to no particular pitch.

arpeggio—playing notes of a chord in quick succession, rather than simultaneously.

drum roll

Chapter Five

Often, directions are placed at the beginning of a passage to define the overall feeling, or mood, of the piece. Below are some common terms.

TERM	TRANSLATION
ad libitum (abbr. ad lib.)	freely, improvised.
agitato (abbr. agit.)	with agitation.
animato (abbr. anim.)	animated.
cantabile (abbr. cantab.)	singing, like a song.
con sordino (abbr. con sord.)	"with mutes," muted; usually for violin or piano.
dolce	sweet, sweetly.
due corde	"two strings," play same pitch simultaneously.
espressivo (abbr. espres.)	expressively.
energico (abbr. energ.)	with energy.
grandioso (abbr. grand.)	in a grand manner.
grazioso (abbr. graz.)	gracefully.
maestoso (abbr. maes.)	majestically.
mezzo (abbr. mez.)	medium, somewhat.
moderato (abbr. mod.)	moderately.
piu forte (abbr. p.f.)	louder.
pizzicato (abbr. pizz.)	plucked.
sempre (abbr. semp.)	always, continuously.
senza sordino (abbr. sen. sord.)	"without mute," usually for violin/piano.
subito (abbr. sub.)	suddenly.
tre corde (abbr. t.c.)	"three strings," release soft pedal (piano).
tempo primo (abbr. tem. i)	resume first tempo.
tutti (abbr. tut.)	all play, everyone.
una corda (abbr. u.c.)	press soft pedal (piano).
unison (abbr. unis.)	all play same part.
vivace (abbr. viv.)	lively.

Sound Production

There are three components of sound transmission: a vibrating source, a medium of transmission, and a receptor. All sound is a result of the generation of sound waves (vibrations), imparting energy to the elastic medium of air within the frequency range perceptible to the ear (20 Hz to 20 kHz). Instruments producing sound electronically eventually move a speaker cone (either in real time or on playback), which at that point is a vibrating membrane.

This chapter is concerned with the manner in which musical sounds are produced. A few general principles will be helpful:

1) The rate of vibration (frequency) of a sound source depends on its mass (length, size, thickness, etc.). The smaller the object, the higher its resonating frequency.

2) Pitch is also effected by pressure and tension on the vibrating source.

THE VOICE

The human voice is capable of wide dynamic and frequency ranges, numerous textures, and great intensity. Excited by air flow (breath), vocal folds in the throat produce audible frequencies whose duration, tone, and articulation are altered by the mouth, tongue, and lips; creating complex recipes, combinations of frequencies, which are interpreted by the human auditory system as sounds.

It could be said that musical vocalizing is speech that has been refined and stylized. The essential elements of both speech and song are vowels and consonants, each producing different acoustic phenomena by different physical means.

Vowels are the sustained pitches for both speech and song. These sounds are achieved when vibrations originating in the vocal folds resonate within the mouth cavity. Movements of the jaw, tongue, and cheek muscles alter the size and shape of the resonating chamber, producing the vowel sounds.

Chapter Six

Consonants give speech and song intelligibility. They are produced by actions of the throat, tongue, and lips that stop the air stream: "Hard" consonants, called plosives, are produced by releasing the air abruptly. Examples are "B," "D," "K," "P," "T". Other consonants are produced by releasing air in a more gradual way—"S" sounds, called sibilants, are an example. However they are produced, consonants give speech and song intelligibility.

AVERAGE SPEECH DYNAMIC RANGES IN DECIBELS

	WHISPER	SOFT	NORMAL	LOUD
WOMEN	30-40 dB	58 dB	63 dB	68 dB
MEN	30-40 dB	60 dB	65 dB	76 dB

When singing, an especially strong soprano often exceeds 100 dB for short periods. The upper limit for altos, tenors, and basses is about 95 dB.

AVERAGE FREQUENCY RANGES (SINGING)
WOMEN

SOPRANO	c' (256 Hz) to b-$flat''$ (920 Hz)
ALTO	f (176 Hz) to f'' (704 Hz)

MEN

TENOR	B-$flat$ (115 Hz) to b-$flat'$ (460 Hz)
BASS	F (88 Hz) to c' (256 Hz)

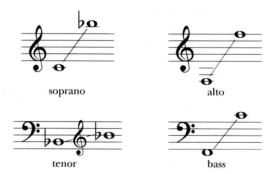

The above frequency ranges are for vowel sounds. Consonants contain much higher frequency information, with sibilants (*s, sh*) reaching frequencies of 10 kHz and above.

Essentials of Music for Audio Professionals

High frequencies tend to be much more directional than the lows, and this is especially the case with speech and singing. In addition, reflections from hard surfaces (like adding reverb/echo), while increasing overall loudness, also tend to blur intelligibility. Consider the difficulty understanding announcements in train stations. High-frequency information (in consonants), arriving directly from a loudspeaker, is mixed with numerous reflections of itself, each arriving sequentially, fractions of a second later, blurring consonant distinction, hence, intelligibility. An overuse of reverberation effects on vocals has a similar result.

PERCUSSION

If the human (or for that matter, animal) voice was the first musical instrument, surely the drum was the second. Percussion instruments include any whose sound is produced by striking, shaking, scratching, or a similar technique. Some of these produce clearly recognizable fundamental pitches while the frequency recipes of others are too complex to be readily deciphered by the ear instantly, and we consider them to have "indefinite" pitch.

Percussion instruments are usually categorized by whether or not they produce definite pitch. Here, they are further classified as membranophones, which are played by striking a membrane (which vibrates to produce sound); idiophones, which are plucked, struck, rubbed, scraped or shaken; and metallophones, pitched percussion made from tuned metal; xylophones; and string/percussion hybrids.

PERCUSSION CLASSIFICATION

MEMBRANOPHONES

INDEFINITE* PITCH	TUNABLE
slit drums	tympani
snare	timbales
tenor	tablas
bass	bongo
tambourine	conga
bodrahan, etc.	roto-toms, etc.

*To an extent these are tunable, but their complex recipes often produce several simultaneous frequencies.

IDIOPHONES	METALLOPHONES
rattles	chimes
vibra-slap	orchestra bells
wood block	celesta
claves	hand bells
afuche	gamelan
ganza	vibraphone
castanets	steel drum
guiro	kalimba, etc.
sleigh bells	
cymbals	
cow bell	
anvil	
spoons	
bones	
jingles	
gong, etc.	

XYLOPHONES
xylophone
marimba
piccolo xylophone
bass marimba
temple blocks

STRING/PERCUSSION HYBRIDS

KEYBOARD	OTHER HYBRID
piano forte	hammered dulcimer
acoustic piano	santur
spinet	

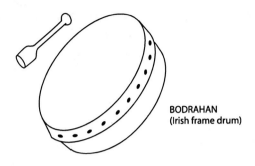

BODRAHAN
(Irish frame drum)

MEMBRANOPHONE

CLAVES
(Afro-Cuban)

IDIOPHONE

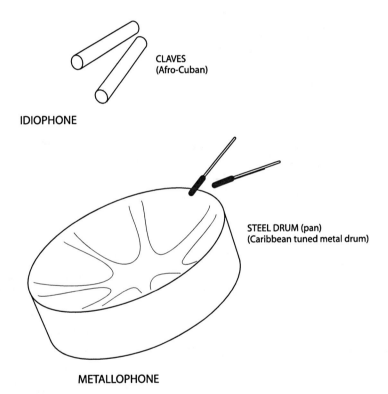

STEEL DRUM (pan)
(Caribbean tuned metal drum)

METALLOPHONE

However their sounds are initiated, all instruments produce a measurable acoustic phenomenon (called an envelope) consisting of attack, decay, sustain and release elements.

In general, the attack is the loud dynamic spike at the enunciation of sound, followed by a decay in level. The sustain is the resonating of the instrument, and the release is the gradual dying away of the vibration. (The actions of gongs, bells, or cymbals are familiar examples wherein all four of these elements are easily recognized.)

The most obvious component for percussion instruments is the attack (compare it to the consonant in speech and song.): Since it carries the most dynamic energy, its timing is crucial in any ensemble playing. The ability to subdivide the beat with precision is mandatory for any percussionist. Although many beat patterns are learned by rote, the ability to visualize these rhythms in notation is a distinct advantage.

It would be a mistake to assume that percussion technique is confined to timing. Each percussion instrument produces a characteristic tone—timbre—as well. This is a result of the interaction between the fundamental vibration frequency and its overtones (harmonics), a process influenced almost entirely by the player's technique.

It is easy to understand that the dynamic range (softest to loudest sound possible) is a function of the force applied, for the most part. Less obvious, perhaps, is the notion that rhythmic accuracy produces the sensation of loudness in an ensemble.

The ear/brain mechanism translates clarity as dynamic level and so it is, since the intensities of in-phase (simultaneous) attacks reinforce one another. An ensemble lacking timing precision, even though its members may be producing a great number of decibels individually, lacks this clarity and seems, somehow, less intense. In fact, many of the frequencies produced are out of phase and, therefore, partially canceled rather than summed.

The frequency range for percussion instruments is quite wide. While tonal (tuned) instruments, like timpani, may produce fundamentals in the bass range and below, the initial attack spikes of virtually all percussion instruments contain complex frequency recipes with partials (harmonics) above 10 kHz. These frequency components are necessary to produce the characteristic textures of the instrument. It is also important to realize that the sound of a percussion instrument emanates from its whole body, not simply from the point at which physical contact is initiated. The shell of the drum, the resonator tubes of the vibraphone, the sound box of the piano, indeed even the material composition and physical dimensions of the stick or mallet comes into play. (As with all sound sources, interaction with the environment is also a major factor. To get a clear sound picture, it is necessary to "stand back.")

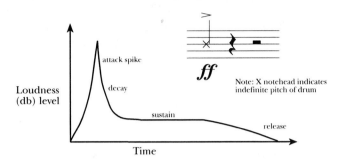

SNARE DRUM: single tap, fortissimo

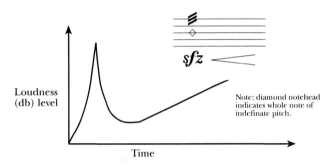

SNARE DRUM: sforzando crescendo roll

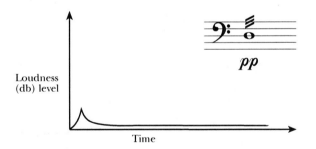

TYMPANI: pianissimo roll

Percussion instruments can yield dynamic levels in excess of 130 dB in the "near field."

Wind instruments are those whose sound is initiated by the the performer's mouth and breath. There are essentially two categories, generally defined not by the material from which they are made, but the mouthpiece they employ to create sound. Woodwinds have a single-reed (i.e. clarinet), double-reed (oboe family) or open-hole (flute) mouthpiece; brass instruments (which are all actually made of brass) have cupped or conical mouthpieces, which produce vibrations directly from the player's lips:

WOODWINDS	BRASS
clarinet	bugle
oboe	trumpet
English horn	cornet
bassoon	mellophone
flute	French horn
piccolo	trombone
saxophone*	baritone
	flugelhorn
	tuba

The saxophone should technically be called a "brasswind," since it combines features of both instrument families

Musicians often use the term "horn" generically, to include all wind instruments. In its specific sense, it refers to the French horn.

WOODWIND INSTRUMENTS

END-BLOWN FLUTES

The earliest instruments of this kind were natural reeds, like bamboo, and the hollowed bones of animals. They had no finger holes, were usually held vertically, and were "end blown;" that is, blown across the upper opening of the tube. The panpipe, made by lashing together a group of end-blown flutes of varying sizes, is common to most cultures.

The addition of finger holes allows for the production of multiple pitches. Opening and closing the holes has the effect of shortening or lengthening the tube, causing it to vibrate at different frequencies—the shorter the tube, the higher the pitch.

Another "technical improvement"* for the end-blown flute is a notched or sharpened edge, which splits the air more smoothly and results in a more uniform, or centered, pitch. The Japanese shakuhachi is such an instrument.

Still another variation is the block flute, which guides air through a passage to the sharp edge. The whistle and recorder are examples of this type, also known as the duct flute or fipple flute.

Note: It is important to realize that instruments simple in construction are not less musical or inferior to those made to rigid technical specifications. They simply produce sounds of a different kind, are often quite difficult to master, and are often capable of frequencies and textures beyond the limits of more "modern" instruments.

SINGLE TUBE FLUTE   AIR STREAM FLOW

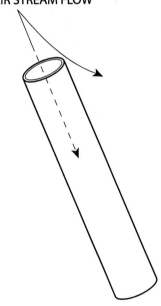

PIPES OF PAN

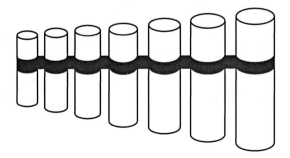

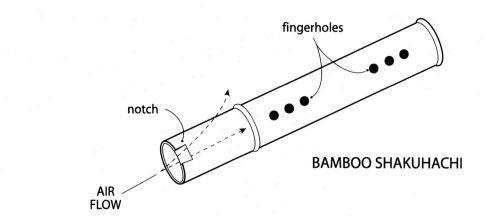

fingerholes

notch

AIR
FLOW

BAMBOO SHAKUHACHI

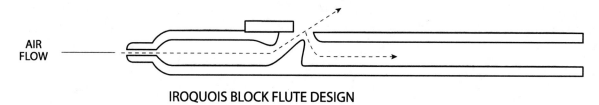

AIR
FLOW

IROQUOIS BLOCK FLUTE DESIGN

AIR
FLOW

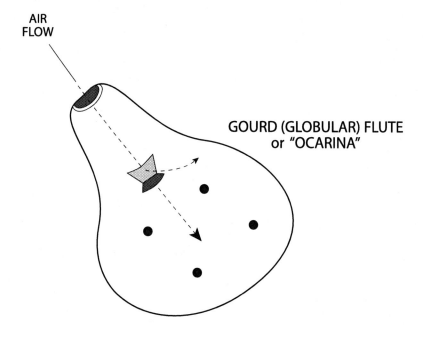

GOURD (GLOBULAR) FLUTE
or "OCARINA"

The name "transverse flute" is often used to describe the modern flute; it also describes the ancestor of the modern orchestral flute, defining the first instruments held horizontally, with sound produced by air blown across an opening on the side of the tube. (The origins of this design appear to be Asian.)

This flute is the ancestor of the modern orchestral type and is sometimes called the natural flute.

ESTONIAN PIIBAR FLUTE

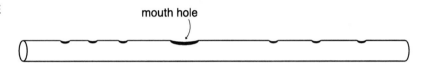

KORA KORA FLUTE OF ZIMBABWE

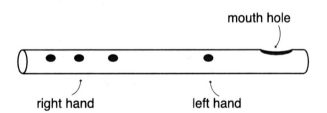

Regardless of design, it is significant that sound emanates via all openings in the flute, mouth holes, and finger holes. This instrument is capable of producing multiple tones with the same fingerings by the technique of "overblowing," rapidly forcing air through the tube and across the opening, which increases pressure and excites harmonic overtones.

This group is divided into two main types, beating reeds and free reeds. The "pitch" generated by free reeds is dependent upon the size of the reed itself within a tube or chamber. This is the operational principle of the mouth organ (harmonica) and accordion.

Beating reeds include all the orchestral woodwinds and this category is further subdivided into single reeds and double reeds. In either case, the sound production principle remains constant: the reed's vibration is initiated by the breath, controlled by muscle tension and air speed, and the pitch determined by varying the effective length of the vibrating column by means of keys or finger holes.

SINGLE REED PRINCIPLE

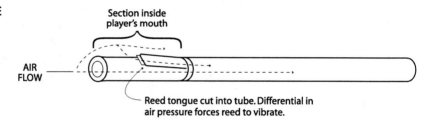

Section inside player's mouth

AIR FLOW

Reed tongue cut into tube. Differential in air pressure forces reed to vibrate.

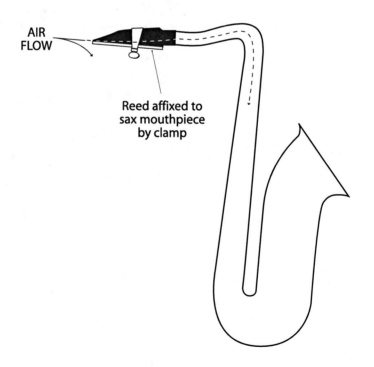

AIR FLOW

Reed affixed to sax mouthpiece by clamp

DOUBLE REED PRINCIPLE

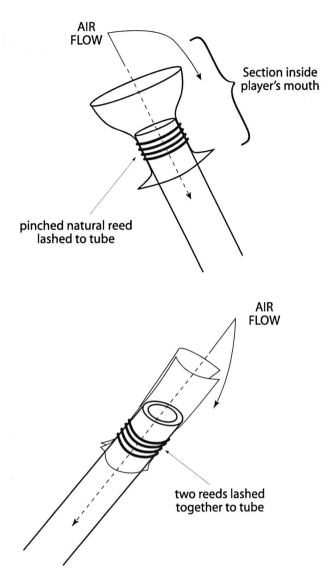

AIR
FLOW

Section inside
player's mouth

pinched natural reed
lashed to tube

AIR
FLOW

two reeds lashed
together to tube

As with flutes, sound exits at key and finger holes, as well as
the end of the tube. Near field dynamic levels will peak at
about 70 dB.

Sound is produced in brass instruments by the vibration of the player's lips, amplified by the body of the instrument; the ancestors of these instruments are conch shells and animal horns.

Each length of tubing, whether conical or cylindrical, has a fundamental frequency at which it will resonate when matched (or even approximated) by the vibration rate of the lips. A spectrum of harmonics (whole-number multiples of the fundamental frequency) are also excited, depending on air pressure. All natural horns (without keys, finger holes, piston valves, or rotaries) are played in this manner. Other examples of this principle are the Australian aboriginal didgeridoo and the long plastic horns played as noise makers at sports events.

NATURAL HORN

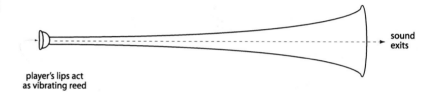

player's lips act
as vibrating reed

NATURAL HARMONIC SERIES
—ORCHESTRAL C TRUMPET

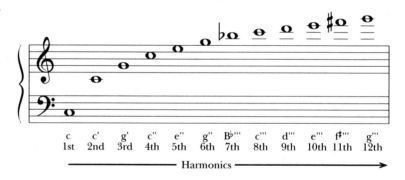

Note: 1) The second harmonic is two times the frequency of the first (producing an octave relationship). The third harmonic is three times the first, and so on.

2) The higher harmonics grow closer together in pitch and eventually allow the playing of half-step increments without the use of mechanical valves, slides, etc. Pitch control is extremely difficult at these harmonics, however.

The addition of a slide enabled the effective length of tubing to be adjusted and other harmonics, based on lower fundamentals, to be accessed, filling in "holes" in lower scale tones. For example, the trombone slide has seven positions, from all the way in (1st) to fully extended (7th).

TROMBONE - slide in 1st position

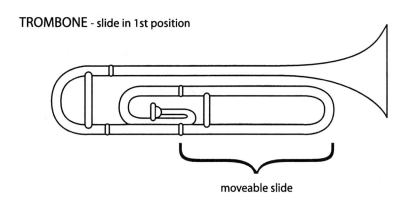

moveable slide

PISTON-VALVE SYSTEM

Pressing the piston sends the air through an additional length of tubing, lowering the resultant frequency; in effect, yielding the harmonic overtones of seven natural horns from one instrument. There are seven possible combinations of the 3-valve system.

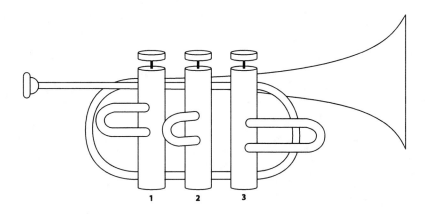

FINGERING COMBINATIONS

1	"open" (valves up)	natural harmonic series
2	2nd valve	all notes lowered ½ step
3	1st valve	all notes lowered 1 step
4	3rd valve (or 1st plus 2nd)	all notes lowered 1½ steps
5	2nd and 3rd valves	all notes lowered 2 steps
6	1st and 3rd valves	all notes lowered 2½ steps
7	1st, 2nd, and 3rd valves	all notes lowered 3 steps

Note: Sound produced by brass instrumens is more directional in nature than that of woodwinds, since it emanates exclusively from the bell. Dynamic levels in the near field can exceed 135 dB.

STRINGS

These instruments produce sound by the vibration of strings set in motion by bowing, strumming, or plucking. The sound is further amplified by a resonating membrane or chamber. Such instruments are sometimes referred to as **CHORDOPHONES**.

ORCHESTRAL STRINGS

Violin

Viola

Violoncello

Bass viol

harp

ADDITIONAL STRINGS

guitar

mandolin

folk harp

strummed dulcimer

banjo

lyre

zither

lute

A string's dynamic level is determined via a system based on string mass, force applied and the size of the resonator. Pitch is dependent on string mass, length and tension. Sound emerges from the point of contact between strings and bow, fingers, or plectrum and also from the surface of any resonator, as well as from within, through openings in the resonator. The following are some examples of string instruments:

LYRE

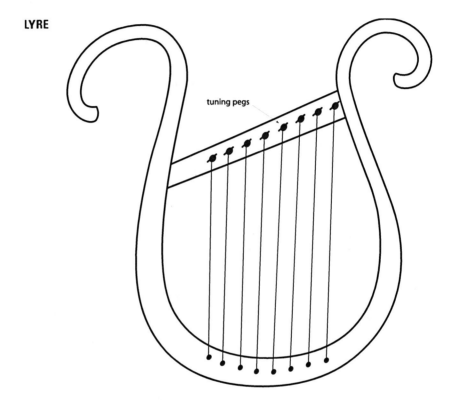

tuning pegs

(Plucked or tapped with stick. Bow bends to alter string tension.)

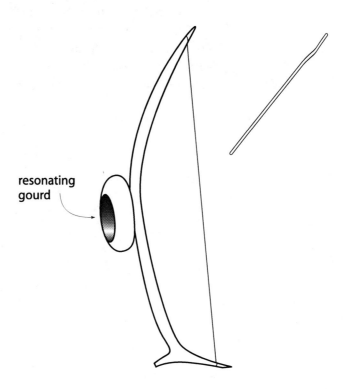

resonating gourd

FIXED OR RIGID BOW

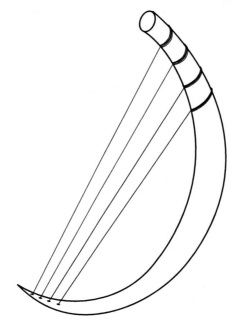

**BOW WITH RESONATOR
(MEDITERRANEAN REGION)**

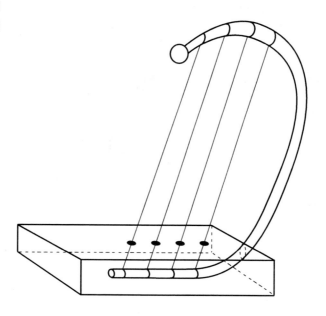

EUROPEAN VIOLIN

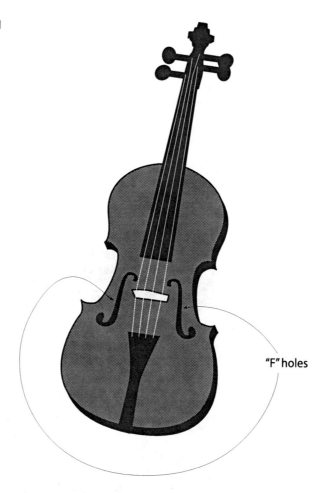

"F" holes

LUTE, 'UD, (OUD) (MIDDLE EAST)

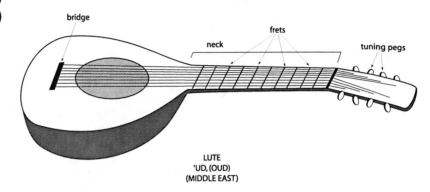

LUTE
'UD, (OUD)
(MIDDLE EAST)

Electric guitars and electric bass guitars initiate sound in the same manner, then a small microphone or "pick-up" (or any combination or array of these) converts the mechanical energy of the vibration to electrical energy. This electrical energy is then amplified and sent to speakers, which resonate to reproduce sound vibrations.

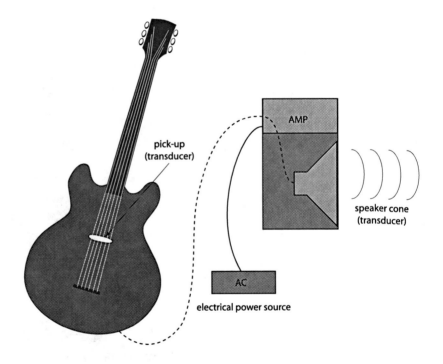

Frequency ranges for various stringed instruments vary. Bass viols can produce 40 Hz at the low end of their range, while violins and electric guitars can reach beyond 5 kHz at the top end. Dynamics for acoustic strings are a function of the force imparted by the player and the resonance properties of the sound box. A violin in the near field may exceed 90 dB. It is important to understand that certain "non-musical" sounds are produced by all instruments, which, though beyond discernable pitch, are part of the characteristic texture of timbre of the instrument. For instance, the bow hair oscillations of a double bass (bass viol) can reach frequencies in the 10 kHz range. These are audible and identifiable and, on a recording, their absence would be conspicuous.

THE PIANO

The piano is actually a hybrid instrument, considered by some to belong to percussion, others to the string family. It is useful, in either case, to understand a little about its mechanism.

The piano is actually a kind of keyboard-activated hammered dulcimer. Felt hammers strike tuned strings, grouped in threes to reinforce the dynamic levels. Their sympathetic oscillations are amplified by the sound board, causing the air enclosed in the sound box to resonate as well. The tremendous combined tension of the metal strings is held by a cast-metal harp within the instrument—the principal factor in the piano's considerable weight. Piano is the shortened term for pianoforte—literally, "soft-loud." Dynamics are controlled by a combination of the force of the key stroke, pedals that lift some strings away from the hammers, and the position of the piano lid. The frequency range for the standard acoustic piano extends from AAA (27.5 Hz) to c"" (4,096 Hz).

RANGE OF THE ACOUSTIC PIANO

RANGE OF THE ACOUSTIC PIANO

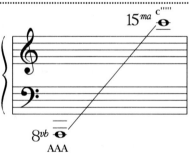

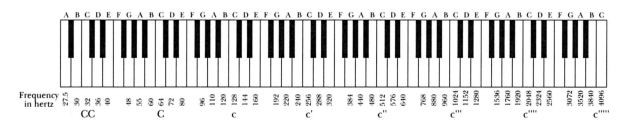

In a sense, any instrument whose sound is passed through an electrical process on the way to the listener is electronic. This definition could extend to any electrical device that produces music, like a radio or stereo playback system. Strictly speaking, however, it is generally agreed that an electronic instrument is one that generates tones electrically, by means of a voltage-controlled oscillator (VCO). A VCO is a tone generator whose pitch varies in proportion to the amount of voltage applied to it. Such instruments are properly called analog synthesizers. Other synthesizers utilize digital sampling and processing.

Modern synthesizers are capable of replicating with near accuracy the tone colors (timbres) of most acoustic instruments, as well as a wide variety of other sounds and effects. For synthesizers, dynamic and frequency ranges (in theory, at least) are defined only by the limitations of the playback or monitor systems. Their most common use at present is in commercial music; i.e., television and film soundtracks, commercial jingles, and in combination with other instruments in pop and jazz fusion music.

Composers and arrangers often combine synthesizers with computers and specialized software as tools for writing and orchestration. MIDI (Musical Instrument Digital Interface) is a standard for transmitting digital information containing commands for parameters (sound selection, volume, etc.) for playing back electronic instruments—the digital equivalent of a player piano roll. MIDI is also useful for its recording applications.

One or more MIDI instruments can integrate with a sequencer, a digital device (available as software, within an electronic instrument, or as a standalone MIDI device) that "memorizes" what is played on the synthesizer and recreates the performance on command. Also, horn players, guitarists, drummers, and other players can access synthesizer sounds via MIDI triggers attached to their instruments. Drum machines can be used alone or in combination with keyboard synthesizers to create a great variety of sonic effects.

New technologies have continually been applied to the making of music, and have usually met with a combination of acceptance and resistance. The keyed system for flutes expanded the capabilities of the instrument, but also changed its sound. Making flutes from metal rather than wood further altered the timbre of the instrument. These developments are neither positive or negative; but, rather, completely subjective and utilitarian. As large ensemble music became the norm throughout Europe and composers traveled between major urban centers, standardization and uniformity became priorities for instruments. Still, modern synthesizers are often programmed to imitate wood flutes, steel drums, and other "low tech" sound sources.

In context, the sounds of these "simple" instruments, the instruments themselves, and the musicians who play them are as musically valid as they ever were.

Essentials of Music for Audio/Video Professionals

Melody

Melody is a term with a number of acceptable definitions:

A horizontal musical line of notation on the staff
A succession of rhythms and pitches
A tune

A useful device for the concept is this analogy: Melody is to a musical work what a paragraph is to a composition. No definition will be perfect. Clearly, the melody is a usually linear subdivision of a larger work, but what are its parameters? Where does it start or end? Can a musical piece have more than one melody?

These questions are answered in a variety of ways, depending on cultural context and a concept called "common practice."

The melody of plainsong, a single-line liturgical vocal music of early European medieval times, might encompass the entire piece. The melody of Duke Ellington's "C-Jam Blues" consists of a four-measure phrase, repeated three times and using only two discrete pitches, *G* and *C*. The melody of Antonio Carlos Jobim's "One-Note Samba" actually contains most of the chromatic scale. Yet, all of these examples have a certain recognizable unity of form and each answers the question, "How does the song go?"

AUDIO SAMPLE 12

Chimes of London, (trad.) David Ladd, flute.

Chimes of London   Traditional

Note: When note heads are above the middle horizontal line ("B" in the treble clef), the stems point downward and are attached to the left of the head; notes above the middle line have stems on the right, pointing upward. Notes falling on the middle line can be written either way.

This example is familiar as the common Big Ben bell tune rung on the hour. Note its visual (and aural) symmetry, and its feeling of resolution or repose on the last tone. Four different pitches are used. With the exception of the order of the notes in measure 5, the second four measures are identical to the first four. The concept of repetition is important in musical composition.

AUDIO SAMPLE 13

Turkish March (*Mozart*) David Ladd, flute.

March   MOZART

Note repeat signs. (See Chapter 3) Six different pitches are used, and there is a discernable visual and audible shape, or contour, in this melody.

AUDIO SAMPLE 14

ROW, ROW, ROW YOUR BOAT (trad.) David Ladd, flute.

Row, Row, Row Your Boat   Traditional

The range of this melody is one octave *(d' to d")*. The contour rises to its highest pitch at measure 5, then returns to its starting note in the last measure.

Some melodies are constructed in two distinct sections, usually classified as A and B, respectively (for more on form, see Chapter 8):

Chapter Seven   **69**

"Pop Goes the Weasel" (trad.) David Ladd, flute.

Pop Goes the Weasel   Traditional

Another pattern is **A-B-A**:

"Goin' Home" (trad.) David Ladd, flute.

Symphony in E Minor: "New World"   DVORAK
Second Movement

Some melodies comprise **A-B-C** or **A-A-B-C** form:

"Hatikvah" (Israeli folk song) David Ladd, flute.

Hatikvah

Israeli Folk Song

Most of these examples have their origins in the oral/aural tradition. They were not composed to conform to a particular pattern and were being performed long before they were ever written in notation form. These forms or patterns are merely observations by people who sought to analyze musical structures. Of course, music is often written according to an established formula: Pop songs, concertos, symphonies, and the blues all have certain structural forms that have become common practice, but these patterns are simply formalized versions of melodic construction techniques common to oral cultures, and these constructs were arrived at simply because they sounded good and felt right to singers and players who learned them by rote.

REFINED DEFINITION:

- A melody is a series of discrete pitches moving sequentially through time and perceived as a unit.
- A phrase is a musical fragment of melody, a musical thought. If the melody is analogous to a paragraph, the phrase is a sentence. Generally, a phrase is a section performed in one breath by a vocalist or wind player.

Some common practices have developed in the organizational structure of musical composition. In general, the following patterns of melodic symmetry occur:

HORIZONTAL Regardless of time signature, tempo, or rhythm, musical ideas are usually grouped in some multiple of four measures (8, 12, 16, etc.)

VERTICAL If the melody rises in contour, it subsequently falls.

CYCLICAL There is a beginning, a middle, and an end—an identifiable start, movement away, and conclusion or return.

These conventions make it relatively easy to identify the components of a composition by sound and/or sight. In addition, they provide a framework for new composition.

The brain is a mechanism for recognizing patterns. It continually seeks them and will attempt to impose a pattern even when there is none.

PATTERN RECOGNITION

Listen for the melodic subdivisions in the following recorded example:

AUDIO SAMPLE 18

"Belize" (Ladd) David Ladd's Downtown All-Stars; from *Downtown*, (produced by David Ladd, Mike Renwick and Scotty Smith. JazzLadd Records, CDC 1001)

THE SCORE

A musical score is a notation containing of all the individual instrumental and/or vocal parts of a composition, serving as a visual aid to a conductor, producer, engineer, or anyone interested in following an ensemble's musical progression. Score reading is essential for the musician and highly useful for the producer and sound/recording engineer. The musical experience of any listener is enhanced by his or her ability to follow the score.

In the horizontal perspective, the score is a kind of road map indicating sequential events over time. When synchronizing music to film or video, elapsed time and frame counts are inscribed directly on the music to facilitate the matching of sound and sight. Letters, numbers, and symbols of various kinds are used as visual aids and to indicate subdivisions. These markings appear on the musicians' individual parts as well.

Letters are used to indicate large segments of the work. The individual part (or lead sheet) might look like this:

Here, the first violin rests for the entire 64 measures of letter A and enters on a whole note at letter B. The full score would show 64 individual measures of rest for this part, assuming other instruments played during that period.

Numbers can be used in two ways: to indicate large segments, in the same way that letters are used; or sequentially, to identify individual measures. The latter is more common in popular music.

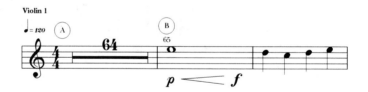

Sometimes every measure of the score will be numbered, but it is more common to place numbers only at the beginnings of significant phrases.

Symbols are notations in musical shorthand indicating precise directions.

SYMBOL   **TRANSLATION**

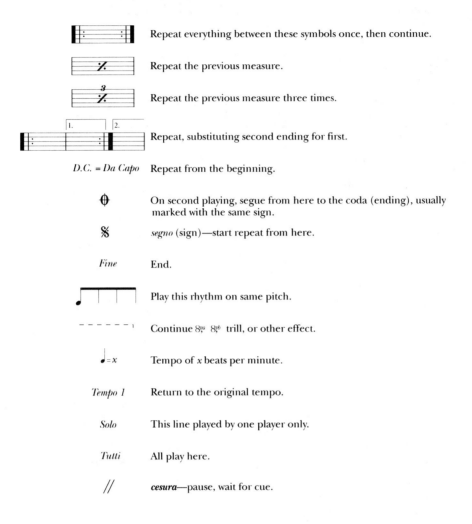

Repeat everything between these symbols once, then continue.

Repeat the previous measure.

Repeat the previous measure three times.

Repeat, substituting second ending for first.

D.C. = Da Capo   Repeat from the beginning.

On second playing, segue from here to the coda (ending), usually marked with the same sign.

segno (sign)—start repeat from here.

Fine   End.

Play this rhythm on same pitch.

Continue 8va 8vb, trill, or other effect.

♩=*x*   Tempo of *x* beats per minute.

Tempo 1   Return to the original tempo.

Solo   This line played by one player only.

Tutti   All play here.

//   *cesura*—pause, wait for cue.

Numbers, letters, and symbols facilitate identifying precise instants or segments in the composition. However, they do not cover every possible musical direction. Often the composer will give a straightforward verbal direction: "tap bow on stand," "howl at the moon," etc.

SCORE ANALYSIS

The following is the score for a section of a brass band arrangement of J.S. Bach's well-known composition Toccata and Fugue in D Minor.

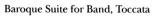Baroque Suite for Band, Toccata

J.S. BACH
Arr. F. DORRITIE

Chapter Seven

75

Essentials of Music for Audio Professionals

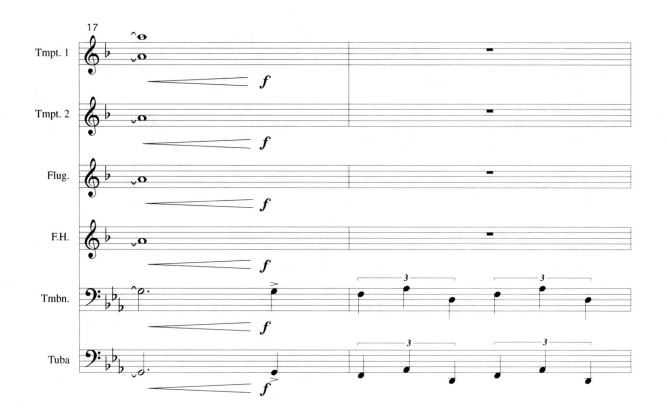

DETAILED ANALYSIS

1. Number and types of instruments—The art of orchestration is the process of matching the music to available instrumentation. In a large ensemble like this, doubling (several instruments playing the same part) is common. This has the effect of reinforcing and emphasizing important melodic ideas. In the preceding example, the first melody is doubled by 1st trumpets, 2nd trumpets, flugelhorns, and French horns. At bar four the 1st trumpets release, and trombones begin doubling.

2. Distribution pattern on the page—Within the sections, hierarchy is basically top to bottom by range. A full orchestral score is normally printed with woodwinds at the top, then brass (often with French horns above trumpets—an example of "common practice") percussion next, with string parts at the bottom.

3. Tempo indication—In this case, a metronome marking is used: 90 beats per minute.

4. Key signatures—Several are indicated since many instruments and are built upon fundamental pitches other than *C*. These are transposing instruments. For example, when a *B-flat* trumpet plays its fundamental pitch, its "*C*," the resulting sound is actually a *B-flat*. The trumpet is built one step lower than true, or concert, pitch; therefore, to sound a true *C*, the trumpet must play one step higher, a note it reads as *D*.

The obvious question is: "Why do we not build all instruments in the same key and avoid all this transposition?" There are several reasons. First, common practice. Large orchestral ensembles are a relatively recent development in the history of music and so is the standardization of tuning. That fundamental *B-flat* of the trumpet might have been a *C* at certain times and places in the past.

In fact, instruments can be, and are, built in any key. There are *C* versions of the cornet (trumpet) that are commonly used in symphony and opera. But the different keys have subtly different textures, and these differences actually help to make the various instruments stand out a bit within a large ensemble. If all instruments were in *C* (concert pitch), reading and writing music would be simplified, certainly. But the various instruments would blend so well that some of their individuality of texture (timbre) would be lost, and distinctions between their voices would be blurred.

Other factors include strong (easy to play) and weak notes of the harmonic series in certain instruments, and the availability of literature for instruments in various keys.

Concert pitch (non-transposing) instruments include:

all strings

flute, piccolo

oboe

bassoon

trombones

baritone horns (in bass clef)

tubas

timpani

all keyboards

5. Time signature—In this case, four-four. Each measure contains four beats, with the quarter note as the metric unit. The strong pulse is on beat one.

6. Verbal directions—These happen throughout. For example: "play what the 2nd trumpets play"

7. Symbols—Used sparingly here:
Cesura (double slash, bar 13): "after release, wait for conductor's downbeat."

8. Articulation marks—Indications as to style of enunciating tones, duration, etc. Note the accent and slur throughout.

9. Dynamic markings—Indicators of relative loudness:

- **ff**—fortissimo
- **mf**—mezzo forte
- crescendo marks
- **subito mf**—suddenly mezzo forte

Musical Form

All music has form. Even free-form improvisation has certain parameters: Who will participate? How long will they play? An hour? An evening? A week? Other forms are more common and clearly defined: a lullaby, school song, commercial jingle, pop ballad, blues, folk song, opera aria, symphony, dance groove, etc.

All of these forms have pattern, design, shape, or architecture of some kind. Whether the formulae are intuitive, chosen, or imposed, the common concept in all is the presence of a beginning, a middle, and an end—and on both sides, silence.

THEME REPETITION

A basic device is to begin with an idea, repeat it a few times, and state it one last time at the end:

LET'S GO, BULL DOGS GO, GO, GET THAT BALL

four times

Assigning letters to the sections yields:

A - A - A - A.

THEME AND VARIATIONS

This is actually another form of repetition, whose pattern could be represented:

A - A1 - A2 - A3

where variations on theme A can be achieved by changes in dynamic level, articulation/embellishment, tempo, harmony, etc., while the essential melody remains.

Two or more different theme patterns, used sequentially:

A - B - A

A - A - B

A - B - C - A

etc.

Most pop and folk songs utilize some version of this scheme.

EXAMPLE: **"Arkansas Traveler"**

Arkansas Traveler   Traditional

Observing the repeat signs reveals this pattern to be:

A - A - B - B

STANDARD POP BALLAD

This is an embellished version of the same form:

INTRO OR "VERSE"	A CHORUS	A CHORUS	B BRIDGE	A CHORUS	CODA OR ENDING

The origins of this form can be traced to the Meistersingers of Germany (1450-1600).

It is helpful to realize that musical forms containing lyrics are likely to follow a poem-like "blueprint," and that rhythmic subdivisions often result from the idioms of speech.

TRADITIONAL BLUES

Each stanza (chorus) of this type of folk song follows this pattern:

A - A - B

For example:

A   I sit here thinkin'
countin' fours and twos (four measures)

A   I sit here thinkin'
countin' fours and twos (four measures)

B   I got the dues payin', concentratin'
first semester music theory blues (four measures)

© 1993 Soaring Dove Productions

EXTENSION

A common way of lengthening a musical composition is by combining the "multiple theme" concept with the "theme and variations" pattern.

Binary form, the use of two sequential themes, was quite popular during the Baroque period (1600-1750) in formatting dance music, especially the Minuet. The first theme, which might be repeated, led more or less inevitably to the second, also usually repeated (A-A-B-B). This J. S. Bach minuet consists of two such themes. The treble part is for the pianists' right hand, the bass for the left.

Measures 1 through 16 can be considered the A theme, 17 through 32 the B melody. 33 through 40 are the last eight measures of the A theme again.

The following audio sample features the treble part only, played by a solo flute. Play the sample several times until you can follow the music visually with ease.

"**Menuet**" ("Minuet") (J. S. Bach) BWV Anhang 116, from *Anna Magdalena's Notebook*. David Ladd, flute.

Essentials of Music for Audio Professionals

- Measures 1 and 2 are melodically identical to 3 and 4, 9 and 10, 11 and 12, 33 and 34, 35 and 36.
- With the exception of one note, the phrase in 13 through 16 is identical to 37 through 40.
- 7 and 8 are identical to 31 and 32.
- Note repeat signs at 16, 17, and 40.

Bach's procedures were so influential that they are still in use. It is very important to realize, however, that these structures developed because they sounded right to the composer; the form evolved from the music, not the other way around.

TERNARY FORM

Ternary form uses three themes in a sequence or one theme followed by a second, followed by a return to the first. Around 1750 (the beginning of the Classical Period), the introduction of new dance forms, like the waltz, served to popularize this formula (A-B-A or A-B-C).

Virtually all large-scale works, such as opera, symphony, concerto, sonata, etc., are organized in some variation or combination of these principles. It will be helpful to develop the skill of identifying these forms, both visually and aurally.

SONATA FORM

The sonata is a form of instrumental music developed in the Baroque period, generally written for piano or solo instrument with piano accompaniment. Sonata form is important to understand, since it forms the basis of writing for much chamber music and for many larger works. It is often the design for the opening and closing movements of symphonies.

- **INTRODUCTION** (optional)
- **EXPOSITION**—States principal theme, usually repeated, followed by a bridge passage leading to a second theme, followed by a codetta (an intermediate coda).
- **DEVELOPMENT**—Builds variations and extensions on initial musical elements and a transition to the next section.
- **RECAPITULATION**—Restates principal and subordinate themes, includes a codetta as transition into the finale.
- **CODA** (optional)

THE SUITE

The suite is a collection of relatively short, contrasting, independent pieces. Differences in tempo, texture, key, meter, and dynamics are emphasized. Commonly, three to a dozen segments are featured. A suite is sometimes a combination of themes extracted from a larger work like a ballet or motion picture score. Examples of suites include:

Peer Gynt Suite No.1—Edvard Grieg
Nutcracker Suite No.1—Peter Tchaikovsky
The Planets—Gustav Holst
Suite from *On the Town*—Leonard Bernstein

THE CONCERTO

The concerto is an instrumental musical composition designed to contrast the sounds and textures of a soloist or small group with a large ensemble or full orchestra. Generally, there are three movements (sections) in the sequence—fast, slow, fast. Usually there is an extended solo called the cadenza, providing the soloist an opportunity to display technical abilities. (The first movement of the concerto is often in sonata form.)

AUDIO SAMPLE 20

First Concerto For Guitar And Orchestra (Almeida), Movement 1, cadenza. Los Angeles Orchestra de Camera, Laurindo Almeida, soloist (Concord Concerto Records CCD-2001)

Play the excerpt several times until you can follow the score easily. (This recording received a Grammy Award nomination for "Best Engineered Recording—Classical" [Phil Edwards, engineer, Frank Dorritie, producer]).

Essentials of Music for Audio Professionals

Essentials of Music for Audio Professionals

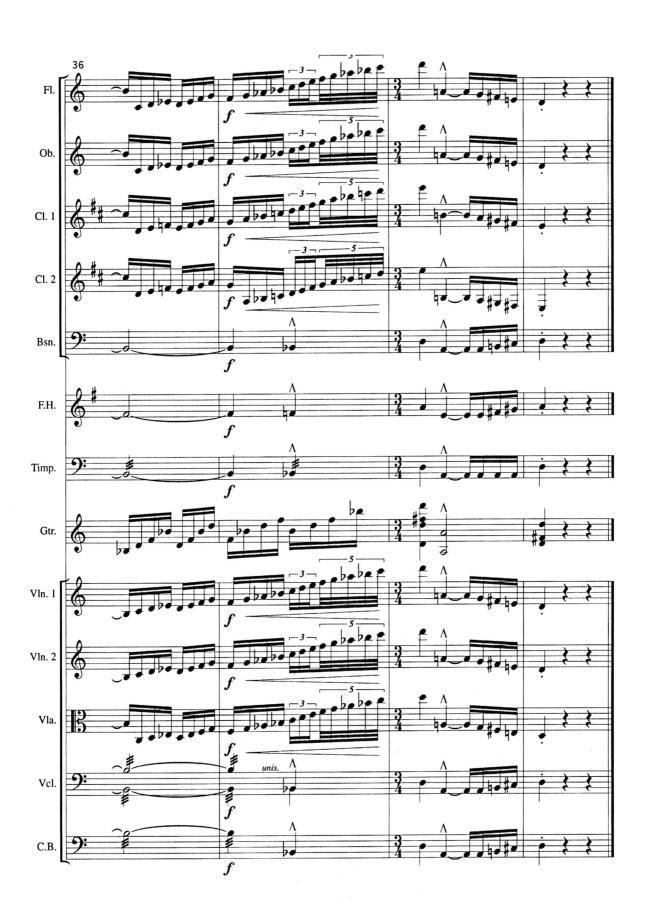

Essentials of Music for Audio Professionals

The symphony is a musical work for orchestra in several movements. This form came into prominence after 1750 and continues as a staple of the orchestral repertoire. Most symphonies have four movements, generally as follows:

- **FIRST MOVEMENT**—usually sonata form, with a moderately fast tempo.
- **SECOND MOVEMENT**—contrasting in dynamic and key, slower in tempo.
- **THIRD MOVEMENT**—further contrast, often in the form of a dance. Usually the shortest movement.
- **FOURTH MOVEMENT**—Usually fast, in sonata or rondo form, returning to the original key.

Some musicologists suggest that the symphony is the ultimate achievement of Western music. Certainly this musical form is most impressive in terms of its scope—the number of performers, range of instrumentation, variety of sonic possibilities available from combinations of brass, strings, percussion, and woodwinds. Composers have sometimes used large vocal choruses and soloists within symphonies. Notable examples are Beethoven's ninth symphony and Mahler's eighth symphony.

SIGNIFICANT SYMPHONIC COMPOSERS

CLASSICAL ERA COMPOSERS (1750-1800)
- Joseph Haydn
- Wolfgang Mozart

ROMANTIC ERA COMPOSERS (1800-1900)
- Ludwig van Beethoven
- Johannes Brahms
- Anton Dvorák
- Gustav Mahler
- Felix Mendelssohn
- Peter Tchaikovsky

MODERN COMPOSERS (20th Century)
- Benjamin Britten
- Edward Elgar
- Charles Ives
- Walter Piston
- Dimitri Shostakovich
- William Walton
- Ralph Vaughan Williams
- Aaron Copeland

This compositional concept is based on the notion that music can be visually, as well as emotionally, evocative. Popular especially since the 19th century (although there are earlier examples, like Vivaldi's *The Four Seasons*), this form might be called descriptive music, as it is meant to suggest or describe a non-musical (i.e. visual, literary) idea. Sometimes it is referred to as a tone painting or tone poem, and can be scored for any size ensemble. Usually, the title is suggestive and/or descriptive, and the program notes are supplied to the audience. Often, nature sounds (bird calls, etc.) are imitated by instruments and sonic effects are common. Program music can assume virtually any structural form, and examples range from solo piano pieces to full orchestra works.

Some notable examplesof program music include Gustav Holst's *The Planets*, Hector Berlioz's *Symphonie Fantastique*, Franz Liszt's *Les Preludes*, Modeste Mussorgsky's *Pictures at an Exhibition*, and *An American in Paris* by George Gershwin.

AUDIO SAMPLE 21

"Jupiter Chorale" from *The Planets* The Santa Clara Vanguard Drum and Bugle Corps, from *State Of The Art* (Soaring Dove Productions)

OPERA

Opera is a large-scale merger of drama and music, usually, a play or story that is sung, with orchestral accompaniment. This form contains a wealth of information for anyone whose interest lies in combining the audio and the visual elements of art; the long-form music video artist, director, and producer, for example.

Musical drama is not a new idea. The ancient Greeks and a host of non-Western peoples, like the African *griots*, included music in dramatic presentations. The emphasis in opera, however, is on the music rather than the action or dialogue, and this tendency began during the Renaissance period in Italy.

The re-discovery of classical models in all the arts led to revivals of classic Greek tragedies, complete with musical components. In 1607, Claudio Monteverdi produced *Orfeo*, a music/drama based in Greek mythology, that is generally considered the first major opera. It featured a prominent role for the orchestra and an increased emphasis on singing. The first public opera house opened in Venice in 1637.

The components of traditional opera are precisely those of the music video:

- **MUSIC**—vocal and instrumental.
- **DRAMA**—plot/story line.
- **COSTUME**—clothing designed for effect.
- **DANCE**—movement and gesture.
- **LIGHTING**—enhancing the action and aiding the "suspension of disbelief."

OPERA TERMINOLOGY

Libretto	The text of a dramatic musical work.
Recitative	Fragments of dialogue, or musical narration.
Recitativo Secco	"Dry recitative" —narration with minimal musical accompaniment.
Aria	Vocal solo with accompaniment; a dramatic musical moment in song.
Principals	The essential cast roles, the lead singers.
Subordinates	The supporting cast members.
Chorus	Singers performing as a group.
Supernumeraries	Extras, non-singing participants.

OPERA STYLES	EXAMPLES
Grand Opera (opulent, spectacular)	*Aida*—Guiseppi Verdi *Tannhauser*—Richard Wagner
Opera Buffa (farcical, satirical)	*The Marriage of Figaro*—Wolfgang Mozart *The Barber of Seville*—Gioacchino Rossini
Opera Comique (dramatic, not comical)	*Carmen*—Georges Bizet *Tales Of Hoffmon*—Jacques Offenbach
Opera Seria (mythological themes)	*Rigoletto*—Guiseppi Verdi *Oedipus Rex*—Igor Stravinsky
Operetta (light, simple)	*Die Fledermaus,* Johann Strauss *Mikado,* A. Sullivan
Singspiel (German language)	*Abduction From the Seraglio*—Wolfgang Mozart *Fidelio*—Ludwig van Beethoven

Note: Other intermediate categories are recognized, and some of these even overlap at times.

The following is an example of an aria:

AUDIO SAMPLE 22

Panis Angelicus (Franck) Franc D'Ambrosio, tenor, with the San Francisco Boys Chorus and the Marin String Quartet. From *Christmas Center Stage* (Rose Louise Productions/Cabana Boy Records)

OPERA FORMAT

Like traditional drama, opera usually comprises three acts. Other elements in opera structure are:

- **OVERTURE**—Precedes Act I. An instrumental piece with fragments or excerpts from melodic themes that will follow.
- **PRELUDE**—short instrumental introductions to Acts II and III. Sometimes called **ENTR'ACTE**.

Forms such as the musical comedy, operetta, rock opera, etc. are direct descendants of the opera. Traditional operas have been re-staged and designed for the film and video media, as well. (A contemporary version of Mozart's *Cosi Fan Tutte*, directed by Peter Sellars, sets the plot action in a roadside diner on an interstate highway.)

THE BALLET

The ballet brings together, in a formal combination, the disciplines of dance and music in the European tradition. This is a court dance, refined and elevated to high social status by Renaissance monarchs like Louis XIV of France, the "Sun King," who actually appeared as a principal dancer in spectacular royal entertainments, thus establishing himself as the center of culture as well as power. Although numerous pieces of music have been created specifically for dance, it is also common practice to adapt works written for other purposes to the singular needs of the dance company. In truth, music and dance have always been connected; the idea of ballet simply formalizes the union. As with opera, an understanding of the principles of ballet will provide the music video artist with a wealth of source material.

- **OVERTURE OR INTRODUCTION**—Quite short in comparison to musical pieces without dance as a focus.
- **SEQUENTIAL "DANCES"**—These will be some combination of pieces featuring a solo dancer, a couple (*pas de deux*), a selected group, and the entire dance ensemble.
- **FINALE**—A dramatic visual/musical culmination.

A story line or plot is usually present. Consider Tchaikovsky's *The Nutcracker*, or Stravinsky's *The Firebird*.

Dance music can be written or chosen simply for its appropriateness and appeal to the choreographer or dancer, and need not have a story as such.

Music for ballet, like music for film, is often groundbreaking and adventurous. An audience may be much more accepting of musical innovation when it is presented with a visual component. Consequently, music written specifically for dance often stretches boundaries.

Igor Stravinsky's *The Rite of Spring*, written in 1913 for the Ballet Russe, caused a virtual riot at its premier performance in Paris. The combination of the exotic rhythms, melodies, and harmonies of the score, the dancing and choreography of Vaslav Najinsky, and the revolutionary costume design of Nicholas Roerich resulted in an extraordinary uproar of shouting and howling on the part of the audience (a most appropriate response, considering the subject matter: primitive nature worship and ritual human sacrifice). To this day, and perhaps because of this notoriety, ballet often finds itself surrounded by controversy.

This is only logical: Music by itself, however radical, remains somewhat abstract. In combination with stylized or ritualized body movement it becomes blatantly real, often sensual. Humans are the only creatures that have difficulty understanding dance as a throwing off of inhibition, either for pure emotional release, or as a prelude to mating.

CHAPTER 9

Harmony, Harmonics, and Sound in Space

Harmony is the term given to the vertical relationships that exist among groups of pitches or frequencies occurring at the same time (as opposed to melody, which defines the relationship among successive or sequential pitches). In musical terms, this relationship is expressed as an interval, a measurement of distance based on a tone's position (order) in a scale. A doubling of any frequency results in an interval known as an octave.

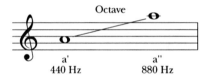

A scale is a succession of pitch subdivisions within an octave; these subdivisions are scale degree intervals. The octave is subdivided in a variety of ways in different cultures (see Chapter 10, MODES AND SCALES).

By and large, Western music employs the diatonic scale, based on seven tones (the eighth being the octave); and the chromatic scale, based on twelve equal increments known as semitones or half-steps. The "do-re-mi…" scale most of us learn in childhood is a diatonic major scale. It consists of increments, some of them whole steps, some half, that comprise the basic nomenclature of musical intervals:

C-MAJOR SCALE

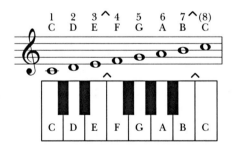

Note the absence of a black key between *E* and *F* and between *B* and *C* on the piano keyboard. These are half-steps (semitones).

The sequential numberings are known as scale degrees. *D* is the second degree of the *C* scale, *E* the third, and so on.

C-CHROMATIC SCALE

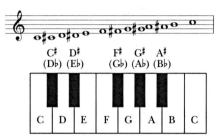

Inclusion of half-steps—here, the notes on the black keys—results in the chromatic, or twelve-tone scale. Depending on context, these are known by either their sharp or flat names; but regardless of notation, they sound the same. Notes that have two distinct names representing the same pitch (i.e. G-sharp/A-flat) are called enharmonic. Harmonic intervals are identified either by numerical or specific names.

Certain intervals are virtually universal, appearing in all musical systems of all cultures. These are the unison (two or more tones of matching frequency), the perfect fourth (first and fourth degrees of the scale), perfect fifth (first and fifth degrees) and perfect octave (a given frequency and its double).

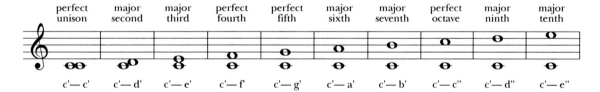

Intervals wider than an octave are called compound intervals. A ninth is a compound second, a tenth a compound third, and so on.

Depending on how pitches are notated, enharmonic interval values have different names. The interval from *C to D-sharp* is an augmented second. If written *C to E-flat,* it is a minor third, for instance. Refer to the following notation:

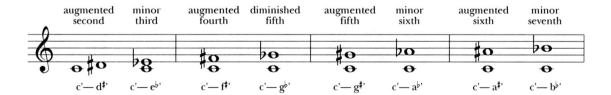

A major interval reduced by a half-step becomes a minor interval:

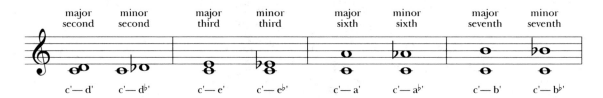

Major or perfect intervals increased by a half-step become augmented intervals:

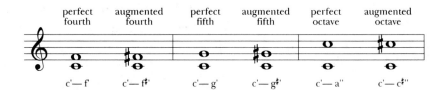

Technically, a perfect interval reduced by a half-step or a major interval reduced by a whole-step become diminished intervals. This latter term is usually applied only to the fifth, however, since the others constitute previously designated intervals.

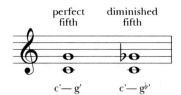

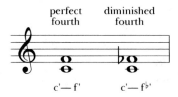

In this case, *F-flat* is actually *E,* creating the sound of a major third.

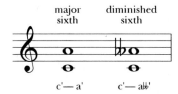

Here, *A-double-flat* is actually *G*, creating the sound of a perfect fifth. Following is a chart of pitch relationships and the intervals they produce:

PITCH	TO	PITCH		INTERVAL
c	to	c	=	PERFECT UNISON
c	to	c♯/d♭	=	augmented unison/minor second
c	to	d	=	major second
c	to	d♯/e♭	=	augmented second/minor third
c	to	e	=	major third
c	to	f	=	PERFECT FOURTH
c	to	f♯/g♭	=	augmented fourth/diminishd fifth
c	to	g	=	PERFECT FIFTH
c	to	g♯/a♭	=	augmented fifth/minor sixth
c	to	a	=	major sixth
c	to	a♯/b♭	=	augmented sixth/minor seventh
c	to	b	=	major seventh
c	to	c'	=	PERFECT OCTAVE

Study this material scrupulously. The concept of the musical interval is the basis for all modes, scales, and chords. These will be discussed in greater detail in subsequent chapters.

EXAMPLES OF HARMONY IN MUSIC

1. UNISON OCTAVE—simultaneous note-for-note duplication of the melody in another octave. (Doubling or halving any frequency value produces an octave relationship.)

2. MELODY AND DRONE—melody played against a sustained note (reference pitch).

Essentials of Music for Audio Professionals

3. COUNTERPOINT—a contrasting, secondary melody, complementing the first. (This example shows contrary motion: The bass part descends as the treble rises.)

4. MELODY OVER CHORDS—combinations of three or more tones played simultaneously with melody. (These chords are usually combinations of pitches suggested by the notes of the melody.)

5. INTERVALLIC HARMONY—matching note durations spaced at harmonic intervals.

FUNDAMENTALS AND HARMONICS

When an object is made to vibrate at a constant rate of between 20 times per second (20 hertz) and 20,000 times per second (20 kilohertz) in an elastic medium like air or water, the ear membrane (eardrum) will react to the resulting changes in pressure and the brain will document the sensation of sound as a distinct pitch. Some experienced sound technicians can identify these tones with reasonable accuracy as to frequency in hertz. Musicians with perfect pitch can identify the letter name of the tone, by ear. Anyone who has read this far and completed the exercises stands a good chance of doing the same with the aid of a piano keyboard. These people are all identifying the fundamental, the most prominent frequency produced by an object vibrating at a constant rate. All musical instruments produce composite pitches made up of this fundamental pitch and its overtones. The combination and strength ratio of these frequencies are what give each instrument its identifying quality, or timbre.

Consider a simple wind instrument like a pan-pipe. Forcing air through one of the tubes at a certain angle and speed produces a recognizable pitch, the fundamental frequency of vibration for a tube of that particular dimension. If the air pressure is increased, at some point a different pitch (frequency) is produced, higher than the first—an octave higher. Continuing to increase air pressure will result in the production of still another pitch, about a fifth higher than the previous one.

The additional pitches are harmonics, or overtones, whole-number multiples of the fundamental frequency, other vibration rates to which this particular object with these particular dimensions will respond. This series of progressively higher frequencies which can be induced out of an instrument are collectively known as its harmonic series.

Musicians will often use the terms harmonics, overtones, and partials interchangeably. They are not identical, however. Harmonics and overtones are equivalent phenomena, but they are numbered differently. For example, the fundamental is the first harmonic. The next highest harmonic (the second harmonic) is the first overtone to that fundamental. Harmonics/overtones are mathematically related to the fundamental; they are whole-number multiples of its frequency. For example, the second harmonic's frequency is two times the fundamental, producing an octave relationship. The third harmonic is three times the fundamental, etc. Partials include all the modes or components, including the fundamental and its overtones. Sometimes the term upper partials is used as a synonym of overtones.

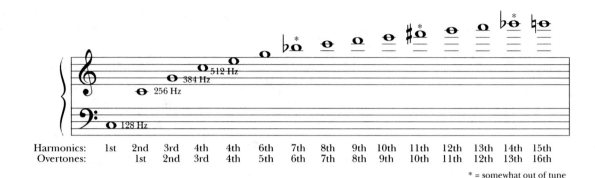

Harmonics:	1st	2nd	3rd	4th	4th	6th	7th	8th	9th	10th	11th	12th	13th	14th	15th
Overtones:		1st	2nd	3rd	4th	5th	6th	7th	8th	9th	10th	11th	12th	13th	16th

*= somewhat out of tune

Note: 1st, 2nd, etc., in this context, do not refer to intervals but to the sequence in which pitches appear in the series.

The blending together of harmonics (overtones) and the fundamental create the identifiable characteristic tone color, timbre, of the sound produced. (Synthesizers use this blending process to achieve close approximations of the acoustic instruments.) The terms tone, timbre, and texture are often used to describe the same characteristic.

If a flute and a French horn sound the identical pitch (frequency), their unique textures will enable a listener to differentiate between them. This is due to the differing amounts of second and third harmonics present in the recipes of each instrument, and the fact that the horn and flute have different fundamental pitches.

Whether in recording, sound reinforcement, or live performance, harmonics are a factor. Their effect on the timbre of the more audible information serves to define and clarify the sound source.

ACCESSING HARMONICS

With many instruments, it is possible to excite overtones to produce varied pitch and timbre.

- **STRINGS:** Lightly touching a vibrating string at its mid-point will produce a pitch one octave higher than the fundamental frequency of vibration (the second harmonic); touching at one-third its length sounds a pitch a twelfth higher (the third harmonic). Touched at one-quarter its length, the string will sound two octaves higher (the fourth harmonic). These notes are generally used as effects.

- **HORNS:** These instruments depend far more on harmonics than do strings. To access the harmonics, the player's lips must vibrate at a rate that matches their respective frequencies.
- **WOODWINDS:** Overblowing (causing an increase in air pressure) can produce the octave and twelfth in some woodwinds, allowing for simplified fingerings. (These are also used as effects in some cases.)
- **PERCUSSION:** Sounds produced by most percussion instruments are extremely complex in recipe. The fundamental pitch, where it is discernable, will outlast the harmonics in duration, though the attack or beginning of the sound may be dominated by partials and overtones.

TUNING PHASE AND FREQUENCY

A musician's intonation is the relative adherence to pitch relationship. In ensemble playing, intonation refers to the comparative relationship among frequencies produced.

In theory, instruments playing together will be perfectly "in tune" when they can match vibration rates precisely across their entire range. They will pulsate at the same rate, in sympathy, in harmony.

If their frequencies drift apart, at some point the relationship will cease to be a unison, but the relative interval between them will not yet have reached a semitone (half-step). At this point, a musician or listener acclimated, or acculturated, to the European twelve-tone system will perceive the instruments as out-of-tune" (out of the tuning system). The frequencies have ceased to reinforce each other and have created a sound event unfamiliar to the listener or player. The sensation of "in tune" (in phase at the same frequency) is produced when, on average, the two instruments agree most of the time within a certain subjective tolerance for variance.

Western music divides the octave into twelve equal semitones (half-steps). These can be further subdivided into 100 cents per semitone. A quarter-tone increment would then equal 50 cents. (Quarter tones are common in Middle Eastern, Indian, and other non-European music systems.) A trained musician will usually tolerate a pitch deviation up to about 5 cents, or 5% of the difference in vibration rate between any two adjacent semitones.

An object vibrating at a consistent rate (frequency) produces changes in the pressure of the air around it. As long as the frequency remains constant, the wave patterns generated will form a regular (repeating) pattern. That pattern consists of a pushing together of air molecules (compression) followed by a relaxation or partial vacuum (rarefaction).

If this were the low *E* string of the double bass, this event would consist of forty cycles of compression and rarefaction per second (40 Hz). Compression and rarefaction are the phases of the cycle.

A composer represents this event like this:

Note: Bass parts are written an octave higher than the actual sound.

The pitch (frequency) produced is *EE* (40 Hz), the lowest possible on the instrument.

The same event could also be visualized this way:

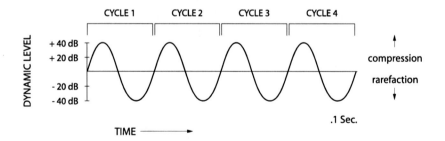

Four cycles are completed in ⅟₁₀ second, therefore the rate is 40 cycles per second, a frequency of 40 Hz.

Dynamically, the wave here peaks at plus or minus 40 decibels, a moderate amplitude roughly corresponding to mezzo piano.

If a second bass were to play along exactly in-tune (or within tolerance limits), the two sounds would reinforce each other:

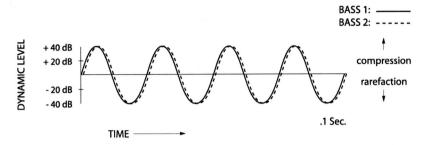

The degree to which they are in-phase, matching compressions and rarefactions per unit of time, results in reinforcement. They are combining constructively, in phase coherency.

The degree to which they become out-of-phase (if one should vibrate at a different rate, for example) will produce partial phase cancellation. In effect, they will be producing wave forms that interfere with and disturb each other's regular pattern.

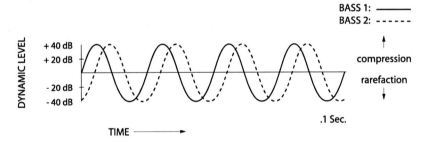

In practice, acoustical phase relationships of perfect coherency or complete cancellation are not possible. Electronic circuits, however, such as harmonizers, phase shifters, and tone generators, can approach these conditions.

Note: The ear seems to perceive clarity as "volume." A certain degree of clarity is produced when instruments are in-tune since their frequencies are reinforcing, rather than partially canceling each other. This is why the in-tune band will be perceived as "louder" than the out-of-tune group, even if the latter is generating a somewhat higher dynamic level.

Essentials of Music for Audio Professionals

It is important to realize that the environment in which a sound is produced affects not only the fundamentals present, but also all harmonics and partials; thereby altering the recipe that produces timbre, the quality of sound. All sounds perceived by the ear are colored by their surroundings. Words spoken at a busy intersection, in an empty handball court, or on a mountain peak will convey quite different sensations even when their inflections and dynamics are identical.

The effect of the surroundings on music is so profound as to be inseparable from, and indispensable to, the music itself. All music is experienced within an audible, acoustical environment, the dimensions and composition of which are vital to the event.

The size of the enclosure, whether it is a small room, cabaret, concert hall, stadium, or even outdoor venues like Woodstock or Central Park's Sheep Meadow (no enclosure at all) is obviously a factor, especially in conveying dynamics. But the composition, shape, and especially, surface materials can be even more important.

Hard surfaces encourage sound waves to bounce back to the listener, reinforcing the direct sound. Soft, absorptive surfaces, such as thick curtains, carpet, acoustical tile, upholstery, and the clothing worn by audiences, will tend to mitigate reflections. Acoustic baffles and reflectors can alter the geometric dimensions of a given space and redirect and/or absorb sound waves.

An anechoic chamber, used for acoustic analysis, is designed to prevent reflections, to the extent possible. This absorptive environment is called dry, as opposed to a reflective, or reverberant, space.

In recording, the illusion of a given space is often created by artificial means called effects, designed to restore a spacial impression.

Many effects produced by the acoustic environment are often recreated in the studio. Echo, a discrete repetition of a sound, is produced acoustically by the environment or electronically by a signal-altering circuit or playback process. Echo is technically a reflection from a fairly distant surface arriving no sooner than 50 milliseconds after the direct sound. There may be one or two repetitions of this event, each diminishing in intensity.

ECHO

Reverberation consists of numerous repetitions of an acoustic event or audio signal, diminishing in intensity but increasing in occurrence over time. This phenomenon is caused by nearby reflections from all surfaces which combine with increasing regularity, building upon each other as the early reflections themselves are re-reflected (reverberation is also recreated with studio effects gear):

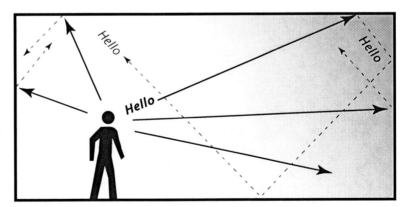

REVERBERATION

These terms echo and reverb are often used as synonyms, but they are not identical, although both are caused by reflection of a sound from a surface.

The absorption and reflection capabilities of a given space are determined by its geometry and the texture and compositional materials of its surfaces. Completely symmetrical enclosures with hard surfaces are sometimes poor listening environments since reflections will follow regular paths and tend to combine into standing waves (the product of reinforced waves, seeming as if the waves are not moving in either direction) at particular points in the room. The enclosure itself is acting as an instrument, favoring certain vibrational frequencies. This creates an imbalance by allowing the room to emphasize certain frequencies over others.

Solutions include altering the shape of the enclosure by placing large objects like baffles or reflectors near walls, facing at various angles, or by suspending reflectors from the ceiling. This will put reflections out of phase by intercepting them and redirecting their energy away from the customary summing or collecting points in the room.

Of course, constructing nonparallel walls and ceiling to begin with is also helpful, but is often avoided on grounds of added expense and visual aesthetics.

Reflected sound is generally desirable, but its dispersion pattern should be somewhat asymmetrical, so it will become more diffuse.

Room geometry can be altered subtly by attaching irregularly shaped molding at random intervals on walls and ceiling, thereby shifting the arrival times of direct sounds and their reflections.

TEXTURE

It is often desirable in relatively small spaces (and, to some extent, in large enclosures) to inhibit the reflections of some frequencies by partially absorbing them where they encounter surfaces.

Soft, porous materials attached to surfaces will absorb and dissipate high frequencies, especially above 1,000 Hz. Curtains and carpets are chosen for these capabilities as much as for cosmetic purposes.

Low frequencies (below 300 Hz) can be partially absorbed with wall panels made in layers. Fabric is stretched on a frame and backed by loosely packed porous material with an air space in between.

Mid-range absorbers (300-1,000 Hz) are constructed by combining porous absorbers with resonating panels of harder material containing perforations.

In any performance space, the audience itself is an absorber of sound. (In many venues, upholstered seats provide the same amount of absorption as would a person occupying them, thus negating the size of the audience as a factor.) *Note: There is no universal absorber that is equally effective at all frequencies.*

It is important to know that reflectors and absorbers are not for elimination of reflections, but for equalizing their combined effects regardless of the listener's position in the room.

The complete elimination of reflection information may be desirable at one stage of the recording process in order to create an effect or the illusion of the performance having taken place in altogether different surroundings. In that event, an artificial reverberation effect is added to the dry signal, thus restoring the notion of a spacial environment.

Modes and Scales

A scale is any arbitrary system of subdividing the pitch relationship commonly known as the octave. Although these systems vary along cultural lines, there are some interval relationships common to virtually all of them. This is logical. Consider a brief look back at the harmonic series of a simple natural horn.

Assume the lowest fundamental of this natural horn (a ram's horn, for instance) is one octave below middle *C.* Here is its harmonic series, the notes a player can produce by varying the rate of lip vibration:

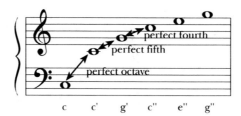

- The first interval encountered beyond the fundamental *c,* is the octave jump to *c'.*
- The next possible pitch is *g',* a fifth above *c'.*
- The next available pitch is *c'',* a fourth above *g'* and two octaves above the fundamental.

Of the first four harmonics then, three are in octave relationships and the remaining interval (the *g'* which is the third harmonic) lies a fifth above its lower neighbor and a fourth below its upper relative. It should come as no surprise, then, to find the intervals of octave, fifth, and fourth in the music of virtually all cultures. The other notes, however, are a different matter.

Modes were basic scales, the first eight of which were approved for Christian liturgical music by Pope Gregory I about 600 a.d., as an attempt to standardize chant. European music of the time was greatly influenced by contact with Middle Eastern culture as a result of commercial trade and, especially, the numerous military excursions of the Crusades. Middle Eastern music, of course, was influenced by Asian cultures and, when the Saracens occupied north Africa and southern Spain at the height of the Islamic Empire, further influences appeared in the recipe.

Modes were utilized as octave divisions and formulae for composition until well into the 17th century, when the present major/minor system based on the Ionian and Aeolian modes, respectively, came into standard use.

These scales are variously referred to as Church modes and Gregorian modes. Each had seven steps and an established final note on which the composition had to end. The modes correspond, step-wise, to the octaves described by playing the piano's white keys only between the notes indicated:

NAME	NUMBER	WHITE KEY EQUIVALENTS	FINAL NOTE
Dorian	I	D to D	D
Hypodorian	II	A to A	D
Phyrigian	III	E to E	E
Hypophrygian	IV	B to B	E
Lydain	V	F to F	F
Hypolydian	VI	C to C	F
Mixolydian	VII	G to G	G
Hypomixolydian	VII	D to D	G

Introduced in the 16th century:

NAME	NUMBER	WHITE KEY EQUIVALENTS	FINAL NOTE
Aeolian	IX	A to A	A
Hypoaeloian	X	E to E	A
Ionian	XI	C to C	C
Hypoionian	XII	G to G	C
*Lorican		B to B	B
*Hypolorican		F to F	B

*These two were rejected by Church authorities, because they contained the diminished fifth/augmented fourth interval, associated with Satan, the *Diabolus in Musica*. The very same intervals, present in the older Hypophrygian and Lydian modes were considered acceptable.

Exercise #▶ 10.1

On any keyboard, familiarize yourself with the sounds of the modes by playing through each one several times, making sure to end on the established final note. No special technique is required. Play slowly. Vary the order of the notes, but always return to the final tone. Write your thoughts or reactions to hearing music in the modal system. What associations do these sounds suggest? Keep your written observation and repeat the exercise several months from now. Compare your observations.

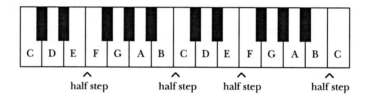

MAJOR SCALES

Success in mastering the concepts of pitch notation and aural recognition flows directly from a thorough familiarity with the major scale. Since the Renaissance, the major scale has been the essential building material for most of Western music, melodically and harmonically, and has become the "language" by which non-Western traditions have been understood in the West. The major scale is neither the most complex, nor the simplest division of the octave. It stands at about the mid-point among all such systems, providing a convenient basis of comparison with, and reference model for, all scales.

The Ionian mode of the Middle Ages and the major scale are identical. The whole and half step sequence corresponds to the pattern from one *C* to the next along the white keys. (Scales can start on any pitch, of course.) Listen to the following example of a major scale.

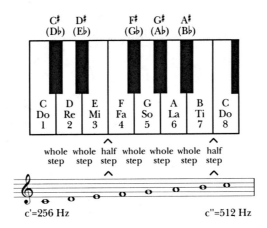

c'=256 Hz   c"=512 Hz

AUDIO SAMPLE 29

C-MAJOR SCALE

In the major scale, half steps occur between the third and fourth degrees, and again between the seventh and octave. Beginning on any given pitch, the superimposition of this pattern yields a major scale whose tonic (reference pitch) is that beginning pitch.

The degrees of the scale are named as well as numbered: (The "do-re-mi" scale, using syllables, is called the solfeggio (or solfège) system. It is part of the oral tradition.)

DO	RE	MI	^	FA
1	2	3		4
TONIC	SUPERTONIC	MEDIANT		SUBDOMINANT

SO	LA	TI	^	DO
5	6	7		8¹
DOMINANT	SUBMEDIANT	LEADING TONE		TONIC

With the information on this page alone, any major scale can be constructed; a major scale can be built from any starting pitch by following the sequence:

WHOLE STEP

WHOLE STEP

HALF STEP

WHOLE STEP

WHOLE STEP

WHOLE STEP

HALF STEP

For example, beginning on *F,* a major scale would contain the following intervals:

F-MAJOR SCALE

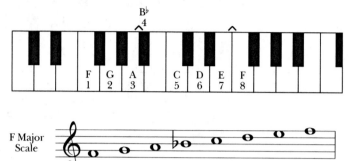

Within the context of this scale, the fourth pitch (subdominant) is called *B-flat (b).* B-flat is the enharmonic equivalent of *A-sharp,* but if we called this pitch *A-sharp,* there would be both *A-natural* and *A-sharp (#)* within this scale, necessitating some means of differentiation.

Following is a list of major scales, with their corresponding intervals noted on a piano keyboard.

BEGINNING ON *Bb*:
Bb-MAJOR SCALE

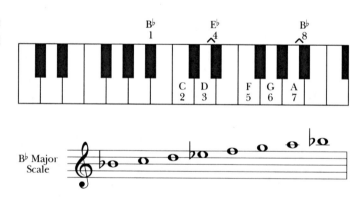

BEGINNING ON *Eb*:
Eb-MAJOR SCALE

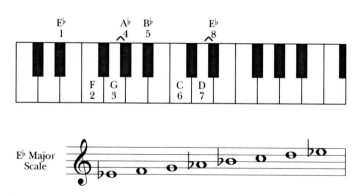

BEGINNING ON Ab:
Ab-MAJOR SCALE

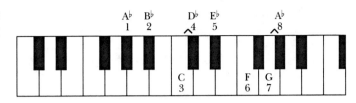

Ab Major Scale

BEGINNING ON Db:
Db-MAJOR SCALE

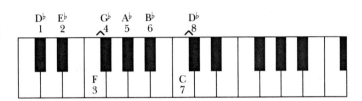

Db Major Scale

BEGINNING ON Gb:
Gb-MAJOR SCALE

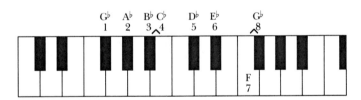

Gb Major Scale

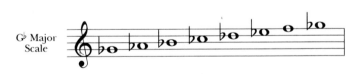

BEGINNING ON *B*:
B-MAJOR SCALE

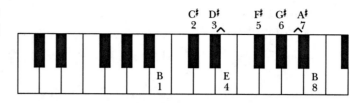

B Major Scale

BEGINNING ON *E*:
E-MAJOR SCALE

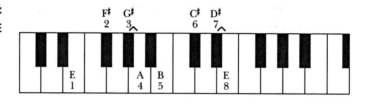

E Major Scale

BEGINNING ON *A*:
A-MAJOR SCALE

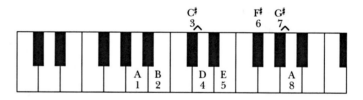

A Major Scale

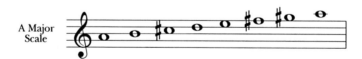

BEGINNING ON *D*:
D-MAJOR SCALE

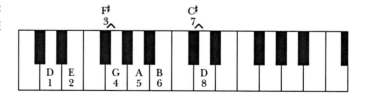

D Major Scale

To avoid confusion, a note and its sharp or flat namesake do not appear in the same scale. That is the reason for calling the accidentals in the *D*-major scale by their sharp names.

BEGINNING ON *G*:
_G_-MAJOR SCALE

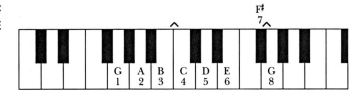

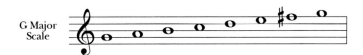

BEGINNING ON *F#*:
_F#_- MAJOR SCALE

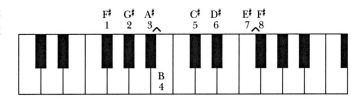

Depending on context, a given pitch may be referred to by its sharp or flat name. For example, the *F-sharp* major scale is identical to *G-flat* major, except pitches are named with sharps:

F#	G#	A#	B	C#	D#	E#	F#
Gb	Ab	Bb	Cb	Db	Eb	F	Gb

In Western music, there are three common forms of the minor scale, each varying from its major scale counterpart, and from each other.

NATURAL MINOR: Differences from the **MAJOR**:
- flat third
- flat sixth
- flat seventh

AUDIO SAMPLE 24

C-NATURAL MINOR SCALE

HARMONIC MINOR: Differences from **MAJOR**:
- flat third
- flat sixth

Differences from **NATURAL MINOR**:
- raised seventh

AUDIO SAMPLE 25

C-HARMONIC MINOR SCALE

MELODIC MINOR: Differences from **MAJOR:**
• flat third

Differences from **NATURAL MINOR:**
• raised sixth and seventh,
ascending only.

The melodic minor is identical to the natural minor when descending.

AUDIO SAMPLE 26

ASCENDING AND DECENDING
MELODIC MINOR SCALES

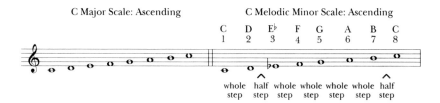

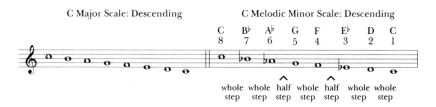

RELATIVE MAJOR/MINOR

Every major scale is associated with a relative minor scale, which utilizes the identical pitches, beginning a minor third below (or a sixth above) the tonic of the major.

This sequences produces a natural minor scale.

AUDIO SAMPLE 27

RELATIVE MAJOR/MINOR SCALES

A-minor is the relative (natural) minor scale produced by using the notes of the *C*-major scale between any two *A*'s. The tonic, or home pitch, of *A*-minor is, of course, *A*.

To identify the relative minor of any major scale, simply include the same pitches, beginning with the sixth degree (submediant) of the major scale.

C-MAJOR/A-MINOR

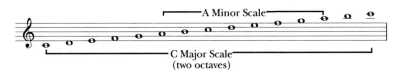

Another method is to descend a minor third (1½ steps) from the tonic pitch of the major, and begin on the resultant pitch. This is tantamount to beginning on the sixth degree (submediant) of the octave below.

F-MAJOR/D-MINOR

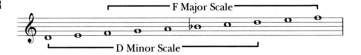

Exercise # ▶ **10.2**

Using the above examples for reference, construct corresponding diagrams for the following (answers are in Chapter 13):

Essentials of Music for Audio Professionals

Major and minor scales are diatonic; i.e., they consist of seven tones. There are several other ways to divide the octave incrementally.

WHOLE TONE SCALE

This is a six-tone division of the octave, using whole steps exclusively. It is considered a "gapped" scale (meaning notes are omitted), compared to the diatonic.

AUDIO SAMPLE 28

C WHOLE TONE SCALE

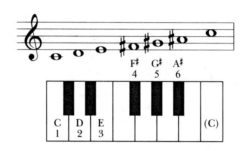

Exercise # ▶ 10.3

Construct the whole tone scales indicated (answers are in Chapter 13):

F whole tone scale

D♭ whole tone scale

E whole tone scale

Dividing the twelve-tone octave by whole steps yields only two combinations of six pitches. In other words, since all intervals are equal, a whole tone scale utilizes the same pitches no matter where it is begun. Starting on *C* yields: *C D E F# G# A# C D E F# G# A# C...etc.* Starting on *Db* yields: *Db Eb F G A B Db Eb F G A B...etc.* Therefore, there are only two mutually exclusive pitch sequences which contain all whole tone scales. The name of the scale depends on the starting note.

BLUES SCALES

This six-tone scale evolved in America as a result of the influence of melodic concepts originating in Africa. It is essentially a method of approximating, in Western tuning, the microtonal (quarter-step) intervals, and others, that exist in the musical cultures of several of the indigenous peoples of Africa, especially those of the North and the West.

This scale is common throughout pop, rock, jazz, and, of course, blues music.

AUDIO SAMPLE 29

C-BLUES SCALE

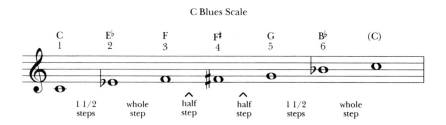

C Blues Scale

Differences from **MAJOR SCALE**:
- absence of second
- flat third
- both fourth and augmented fourth (forbidden by church modes and absent from European major/minor system.)
- flat seventh

Based on the C-blues scale model above, construct the following (answers are in Chapter 13):

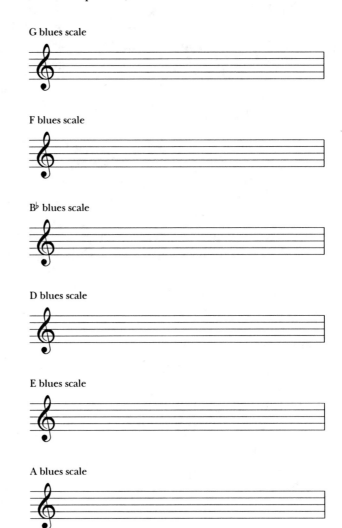

G blues scale

F blues scale

B♭ blues scale

D blues scale

E blues scale

A blues scale

The five tone scale appears in the music of several cultures; Asian, European, African, and Native American. This is a "gapped" scale, meaning notes are omitted.

AUDIO SAMPLE 30

C **PENTATONIC SCALE**

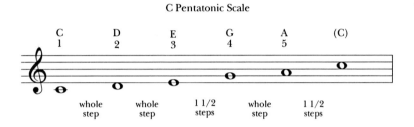

C Pentatonic Scale

Differences from **MAJOR SCALE:**

- omission of perfect fourth
- omission of seventh

AUDIO SAMPLE 31

F# **PENTATONIC SCALE**

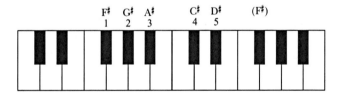

Begun on *F#*, the ascending intervals on the piano's black keys provide a **PENTATONIC SCALE.**

Construct pentatonic scales on the pitches indicated (answers are in Chapter 13).

F pentatonic scale

G pentatonic scale

It is important to realize, in the midst of this scale construction process, that all scales are derived from melodies; in other words, inferred, from common practices within the culture.

The following scales contain nuances not found in Western notation; microtones, for example. Here, then, are some of the countless ways of dividing an octave, approximated in Western notation.

AUDIO SAMPLE 32

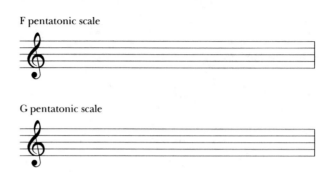

Japanese Insepo Scale
(Edo Period: 1603-1867)

AUDIO SAMPLE 33

Chinese Scale

* Used as passing or subsidiary tones.

(*used as passing or subsidiary tones)

AUDIO SAMPLE 34

Azerbaijani Scale

(Note similarity with Insenpo scale.) This scale is often found in Gypsy and Klezmer music.

AUDIO SAMPLE 35

Ugandan Scale

AUDIO SAMPLE 36

Indian Raga Scale
(Raga Abhogi)

AUDIO SAMPLE 37

Navajo Scale

Gapped scales are scales of less than seven tones (non-diatonic), or those omitting any of the diatonic steps; for example, the pentatonic scale. Altered scales are those containing step substitutions not found in the major/minor system; for example, the chinese scale.

This is the division of the octave into twelve equal semitones (half-steps).

AUDIO SAMPLE 38

C CHROMATIC SCALE

C Chromatic Scale

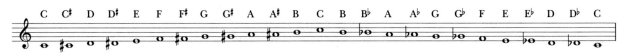

Although the chromatic scale can only approximate microtonal music, it will serve to accurately render any musical sequence within the major/minor system.

Concept of Key

TONAL CENTER

Just as a scale has a beginning and ending pitch, music using those scale tones in any sequence will continue to maintain the same pitch as a center or resolution. The key, then, is nothing more than an arrangement of scale tones around a tonal center called the tonic. To be defined as belonging to a particular key, a given piece of music must gravitate toward a specific tonic. Most music does this in an obvious manner by ending on (resolving to) the tonic in question. Listen to the following example:

AUDIO SAMPLE 44

"Arkansas Traveler" (trad.) David Ladd, flute.

Arkansas Traveler   Traditional

The central pitch, the tonic, is clear to the ear and, if you can follow the music reasonably well, to the eye as well. The tonic here is *D*. The piece uses the notes of the *D*-major scale exclusively, with a resolution on *D*. We can conclude that the key of this piece is *D*-major.

Note the two sharp signs to the right of the clef and left of the time signature. These are the sharps that appear in the *D*-major scale. Here they indicate that, unless otherwise noted, all *F*'s and *C*'s in this piece are "sharped."

There is a direct correlation between the number of accidentals in a particular major scale and the key signature indication of the corresponding key.

A key signature indicates which scales are the essential melodic ingredients in the music to follow. Each key signature can stand for two keys, since both a major scale and its relative (natural) minor share the same collection of pitches.

KEY SIGNATURE CHART

KEY MAJOR/MINOR	SIGNATURE
C/Am	no sharps or flats
G/Em	one sharp: F♯
D/Bm	two sharps: F♯, C♯
A/F♯m	three sharps: F♯, C♯, G♯
E/C♯m	four sharps: F♯, C♯, G♯, D♯
B/G♯m	five sharps: F♯, C♯, G♯, D♯, A♯
F♯/D♯m	six sharps: F♯, C♯, G♯, D♯, A♯, E♯
C♯/A♯m	seven sharps: F♯, C♯, G♯, D♯, A♯, E♯, B♯
	Note progression by fifths throughout sharp keys.
F/Dm	one flat: B♭
B♭/Gm	two flats: B♭, E♭
E♭/Cm	three flats: B♭, E♭, A♭
A♭/Fm	four flats: B♭, E♭, A♭, D♭
D♭/B♭m	five flats: B♭, E♭, A♭, D♭, G♭
G♭/E♭m	six flats: B♭, E♭, A♭, D♭, G♭, C♭
C♭/A♭m	seven flats: B♭, E♭, A♭, D♭, G♭, C♭, F♭
	Note progression by fourths throughout flat keys.

Chapter Eleven

This chart presents the keys, in their natural order. Moving clockwise from *C* in fifths yields the number of sharps in the keys indicated. Moving counter clockwise, in fourths, yields the number of flats.

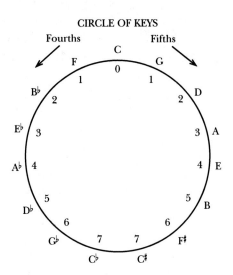

CIRCLE OF KEYS

A practical knowledge of key signatures includes knowing the number of sharps or flats in a given key signature, which notes are altered, the order in which the altered notes appear in the signature, and recognition "by sight" of all key signatures.

MEMORY DEVICES

It is important to memorize key relationships. It has become rather fashionable to relegate memory and memorization to low-order cognitive skills. Actually, they are indispensable. Without memory, you would have forgotten why you are reading this book. Memory supplies a "short cut" for accessing necessary data without having to re-create all the processes that led to its acquisition in the first place.

For example, the phrase **Good Deeds Are Ever Bearing Fruit** contains virtually all the information included in the circle of keys, above.

The first letter of each word, read left to right, indicates the number of sharps present in the key signatures of the keys:

G (1), *D* (2), *A* (3), *E* (4), *B* (5), and *F#* (6).

Reading right to left indicates flats:

F (1), *Bb* (2), *Eb* (3), *Ab* (4), *Db* (5), and *Gb* (6).

One would have to remember that the key of *C* has no sharps or flats, *Cb* has seven flats and *C#* seven sharps.

Neither the circle nor the anagram reveal which pitches are sharped or flatted. This information is vital, and there is a common practice to the order of appearance. Eventually, sight recognition will be achieved, or you may simply memorize each signature individually. At this point, however, an effective method is to memorize a system or pattern, from a given starting point. For instance:

MEMORIZE:

- the key of *G* has one sharp, *F#*.
- the number of sharps and their order (left to right in the signature) progress in fifths.

Therefore, the key of *D* (a fifth above *G*) has two sharps, *F#* and *C#* (a fifth above *F#*). All other sharp keys follow the pattern.

MEMORIZE:

- the key of *F* has one flat, *Bb*
- the number of flats and their order (left to right in the signature) progress in fourths.

Therefore, the key of *Bb* (a fourth above *F*) has two flats, *Bb* and *Eb* (a fourth above *Bb*). All other flat keys follow the pattern.

Still another method for finding the number of sharps and flats in a given major key is to construct the major scale from the tonic. For example:

QUESTION: What is the key signature for *A*-major?

SOLUTION:

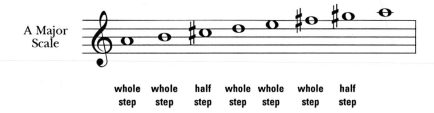

To find the correct order, remember to start with *F#*, and progress by fifths.

ANSWER: The key of *A*-major has three sharps (in order): F#, C#, and G#. They appear on the staff in this manner:

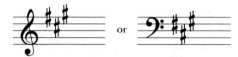

QUESTION: What is the key signature for *G*-minor?

SOLUTION: Find the relative major for *G*-minor by ascending a minor third (1½ steps).

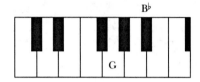

Bb is the relative major of *G*-minor. They have the same key signature (but not the same tonic).

Bb-MAJOR SCALE

For the correct order, start with *Bb* and progress by fourths.

ANSWER: The key of *G*-minor (*Bb*-major) has two flats (in order): *Bb* and *Eb*. They appear on the staff in this manner:

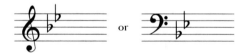

Write the key signatures indicated (answers are in Chapter 13):

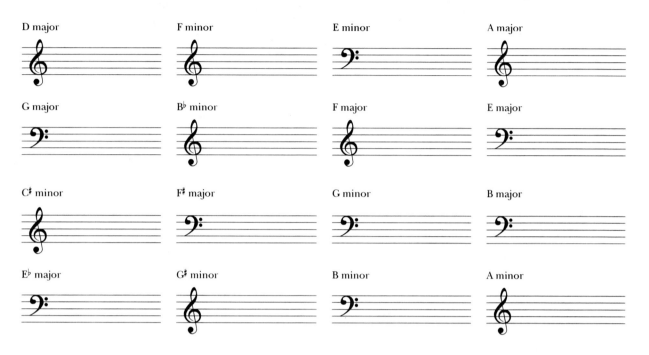

D major   F minor   E minor   A major

G major   B♭ minor   F major   E major

C♯ minor   F♯ major   G minor   B major

E♭ major   G♯ minor   B minor   A minor

Identify the key signatures indicated (answers are in Chapter 13):

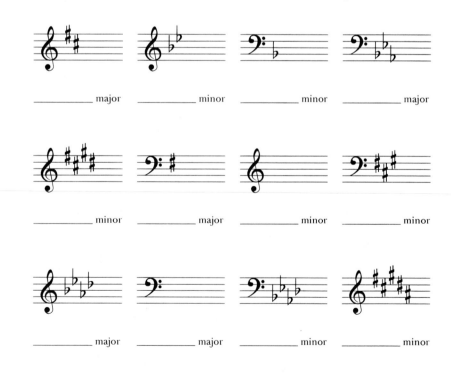

_____ major   _____ minor   _____ minor   _____ major

_____ minor   _____ major   _____ minor   _____ minor

_____ major   _____ major   _____ minor   _____ minor

Essentials of Music for Audio/Video Professionals

Chords

INTERVALS AND CHORD CONSTRUCTION

The distance between two pitches is an interval. A melodic interval defines successive pitches; a harmonic interval, the buildng block of a chord, defines two pitches occuring simultaneously.

This measure shows the octave interval between *C* and *c*.

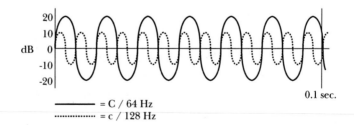

= C / 64 Hz
= c / 128 Hz

This graph represents the same information. It shows a fortissimiso *C* (6.4 cycles after ¹/₁₀ second at 20 decibels) joined by a mezzo forte *c* (12.8 cycles at 10 decibels).

This interval—the octave—is the most common in music. When the audience sings along at concerts, or joins in singing the national anthem at sports events, melody notes may be too high for some singers, too low for others. The usual solution is to sing all or part of the melody an octave above or below the given octave; this technique results in strengthening the melody, since the frequencies tend to reinforce each other. In composing and arranging, this practice is called doubling in octaves or octave unison.

CHORDS AND TRIADS

A chord is composed of three or more simultaneous discrete frequencies. The incidence of three-element chords is common enough to rate its own term: triad.

TYPES OF TRIADS—THE MAJOR TRIAD

Using the *C* triad as a model, construction of a major triad is accomplished by selecting the first, third, and fifth scale intervals from the root (base note of the chord).

Example: *C*-MAJOR TRIAD

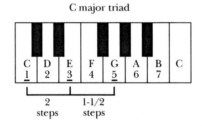

The structure of a major chord, then, is **1-3-5**. Start on any tone, select the tone two whole scale steps (a major third) above and another one and a half steps (a minor third) above that (or, a perfect fifth from the root).

AUDIO SAMPLE 40

C-MAJOR TRIAD

You now have enough information to construct any major triad.

Example: *D*-MAJOR TRIAD

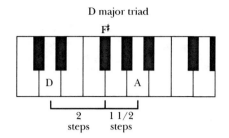

D major triad

Using the 1-3-5 formula, the *D* major triad contains *D, F#,* and *A.*

It is important to realize that there are a couple of ways to conceptualize these ideas. One can simply select the first, third, and fifth degrees of the given major scale.

A-MAJOR SCALE

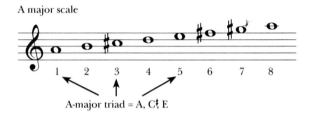

A major scale

Without the context of scale, take the tonic pitch, add the tone two whole steps higher (major third) and another, one and a half steps (minor third) above that, making a perfect fifth above the root.

A-MAJOR TRIAD = A, C#, E

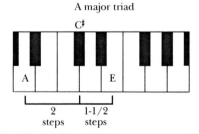

A major triad

 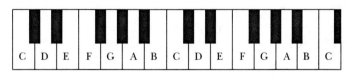

Using the above information as a guide, complete the following (answers are in Chapter 13):

EXAMPLE:

Bb-MAJOR TRIAD		_Bb_ 1	_D_ 3	_F_ 5
Eb-MAJOR TRIAD	INSERT GRAPH	_Eb_ 1	3	5
G-MAJOR TRIAD		_G_ 1	3	5
C#-MAJOR TRIAD		_C#_ 1	3	5
B-MAJOR TRIAD		_B_ 1	3	5
E-MAJOR TRIAD		_E_ 1	3	5
Ab-MAJOR TRIAD		_Ab_ 1	3	5

The formula for the **MINOR TRIAD** is **1-*b*3-5**, based on the minor scale degrees from the root. Begin on a given tone, add the tone one and a half steps higher (minor third), and another, two steps (major third) above that, making a perfect fifth. Or, construct the major triad and flat the third.

AUDIO SAMPLE 41

C-MAJOR CHORD / C-MINOR CHORD

Exercise # ▶ 12.2

Construct the minor chords indicated:

A minor

B minor

THE DIMINISHED CHORD

D minor

D♭ minor

G minor

B♭ minor

E minor

F♯ minor

The common practice formula for the diminished chord is **1-*b*3-*b*5-6**. Begin on a given pitch and add three more tones, each at one and a half step (minor third) intervals.

Or, construct the major triad, flat the third and the fifth, then add the sixth.

_C_-MAJOR CHORD / _C_-DIMINISHED CHORD

Exercise # ▶ 12.3

Construct the diminished chords indicated (answers are in Chapter 13):

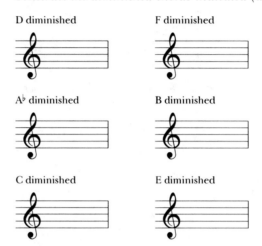

Assuming you have arrived at the correct solutions to the previous exercise you may have noticed the curious phenomenon regarding the names of the tones involved. The *D, F, Ab* and *B* are, in fact, alternate inversions (see below) of the same sequence of four tones (or their enharmonic equivalents). The same holds true for the *C* and *E* diminished chords. (In a sense, there are only three diminished chords, each with four variations.)

THE AUGMENTED CHORD

The formula for the augmented chord is **1-3-#5**. Begin on a given pitch and add two pitches, each at two-whole-step (major third) intervals from the one below. Or, construct the major triad and raise the fifth by a half-step.

AUDIO SAMPLE 43

C-MAJOR CHORD / C-AUGMENTED CHORD

Construct the augmented chords indicated (answers are in Chapter 13):

D augmented

F♯ augmented

A♯ augmented

Notice that these chords are alternate inversions (see below) of the same sequence of three tones. (It could be said that there are only four augmented chords, each with three alternate forms [or their enharmonic equivalents]. To confirm this, construct C, F, and G augmented chords and compare to D augmented.)

TRIADS AND SCALE DEGREES

Triads have different qualities, depending on the degree of the scale they are built on. Examine the following triads:

C-MAJOR SCALE

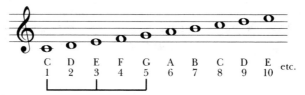

C-MAJOR TRIAD

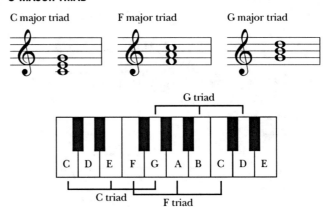

Relative to their home scale, *C*-major in this case, the triads have been constructed from the tonic (*C*), the subdominant (*F*), and the dominant (*G*).

For analysis purposes, Roman numerals are used to represent triads and their scale degrees:

I (major) = the chord whose root is the tonic (the first degree of the scale).

ii (minor) = the chord whose root is the supertonic (the second degree of the scale).

iii (minor) = the chord whose root is the mediant (the third degree of the scale).

IV(major) = the chord whose root is the subdominant (the fourth degree of the scale).

V (major) = the chord whose root is the dominant (the fifth degree of the scale).

vi (minor) = the chord whose root is the submediant (the first degree of the scale).

vii (diminished) = the chord whose root is the leading tone (the first degree of the scale).

So in the key of *C*, the I chord consists of *C*, *E*, and *G*. The IV chord consists of *F*, *A*, and *C*. The V chord consists of *G*, *B*, and *D*.

TONIC	I = *C* TRIAD =	*C, E, G* =	1st, 3rd, 5th scale tones
SUBDOMINANT	IV = *F* TRIAD =	*F, A, C* =	4th, 6th, 8th scale tones
DOMINANT	V = *G* TRIAD =	*G, B, D* =	5th, 7th, 9th scale tones

CHORD INVERSIONS

Inversions are alternate ways of arranging the vertical groupings of a chord's constituent tones.

C-MAJOR CHORD

ROOT POSITION
(1-3-5) *C-E-G*

FIRST INVERSION
(3-5-1) *E-G-C*

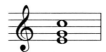

SECOND INVERSION
(5-1-3) *G-C-E*

Voicing is the specific vertical arrangement of harmonics in a musical work. The two major categories are close voicing (intervals spaced as close as they can be) and open voicing (intervals with more space between them), each chosen for its particular effect.

AUDIO SAMPLE 44

EXAMPLE 1. CLOSE VOICING FOR A *D*-MINOR CHORD:

EXAMPLE 2. OPEN VOICING FOR A *D*-MINOR CHORD:

EXAMPLE 3. OPEN VOICING FOR A *D*-MINOR CHORD:

THE SEVENTH CHORD

There are several types of seventh chords, all of which consist of four tones, a triad with an interval of a seventh added on top. These are extended harmonies, as are all chords utilizing intervals beyond the standard triads.

The dominant seventh is the most common form, so much so that when the term "seventh" is used alone, as in "G-seventh," it always refers to the dominant seventh.

The formula for the dominant seventh is 1-3-5-♭7. To build, begin with any given tone and add the tone two whole steps (major third) above, another one and a half steps (minor third) above that, and then another one and a half steps (minor third) above the last. Or, construct the major triad, and add a tone one and a half steps (minor third) above the fifth.

Chapter Twelve   **147**

C-MAJOR CHORD / *C*-SEVENTH CHORD

The use of the term "dominant" with respect to this version of the seventh chord may have more than one origin. Most theory books refer to a dominant seventh chord built from the fifth degree (dominant) of any scale, and including every odd-number-degree tone thereafter. For example, the dominant chord in the key of *C* consists of *G, B, D.* and *F.* Of course, this is not a *C* chord, but a *G*-seventh. Close analysis of the intervals involved reveals the 2 step–1 1/2 step-1 1/2 step (major third-minor third-minor third) pattern described above. This chord is sometimes referred to as the "principal" chord and, to cloud the issue further, it might be pointed out that to construct a *C*-seventh chord, for example, requires the use of a tone that is not in the key of *C* at all; namely, *Bb.*

To recap this convoluted bit of rationale, the dominant seventh chord in the key of *C* is the *G*-seventh, consisting of the tones *G, B, D,* and *F.* A *C*-seventh chord would actually be the dominant seventh (principal) chord in the key of *F,* which contains a Bb, hence its appearance in the C7 chord. Clear?

Still another curiosity is that *Bb* (or a frequency quite close to *Bb*) is the seventh harmonic of *C.* Yet another view is that the particular seventh involved is simply the seventh degree step of the mixolydian mode. If begun on *C,* this mode would yield *Bb* as its seventh step.

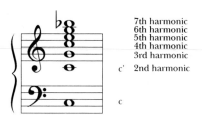

Pragmatically speaking, it is probably best to simply refer to the formula above, 1-3-5-b7, to build the dominant seventh chord, and regard the rest of the methods as examples of the vagaries of common practice.

The major seventh is constructed by the formula 1-3-5-7 (raising the b7 in the dominant seventh chord by ½-step). Begin with any pitch and add the tone two whole steps (a major third) above, then another one and a half steps (minor third) above that, and another two steps (major third) above the last.

Or, construct the major triad and add a tone two steps (major third) above the fifth.

AUDIO SAMPLE 47

C-MAJOR CHORD / C-MAJOR SEVENTH

The minor seventh chord is a minor triad with a dominant seventh. Its formula is 1-*b*3-5-*b*7. Begin with any pitch and add the tone one and a half steps (minor third) above, then another two steps (major third) above that, and another one and a half steps (minor third) above the last.

Or, construct the major seventh and flat the third and seventh.

AUDIO SAMPLE 48

C-MAJOR SEVENTH / C-MINOR SEVENTH

The diminished seventh has the same structure as the previously described diminished chord. The sixth in its construction is really a flatted dominant seventh. Its formula could be re-written 1-*b*3-*b*5-*bb*7.

AUDIO SAMPLE 49

C-DIMINISHED SEVENTH

Color tones are tones added to these basic chord types, enriching harmonic information without implying a change in the basic tonality (tonal center) of the chord. The most common additions are the sixth and the ninth.

AUDIO SAMPLE 50

C-"SIXTH"—abbr. C⁶
(C—E—G—A)
1—3—5—6

AUDIO SAMPLE 51

C-"ADDED NINTH"—abbr. Cᴬᴰᴰ⁹
(C—E—G—D)
1—3—5—9

AUDIO SAMPLE 52

C-"SIX/NINE"—abbr. C⁶/⁹
(C—E—G—A—D)
1—3—5—6—9

This type of harmony appears more frequently in Western music dating from the Romantic period (1820-1910) onward, and was especially evident in the music of Impressionists like Debussy and Ravel. In popular music, examples are found in the compositions of Ellington, Gershwin, and numerous others.

Suspension in harmony is a device whereby a tone is introduced (to serve as a substitute) that is foreign to the established chord. The effect is to create a kind of tension in anticipation of a harmonic resolution or cadence (see below). The most common example is the "suspended fourth." In this case, the fourth degree is substituted for the third in a major or minor chord. The intended result is for the ear to hear the harmony as "incomplete," therefore, unresolved.

AUDIO SAMPLE 53

C-SUSPENDED FOURTH abbr. *C*ˢᵘˢ
RESOLVES TO *C*-MAJOR

(C—F—G)   (C—E—G)
1—4—5   —3—5

CHORD PROGRESSION: HARMONIC CADENCES

A cadence is a chord progression that can be considered a kind of resolution, either a partial or final resting point for a musical statement. Chord progressions will feature resolutions at various points, some suggesting continuance, others, finality.

The question is, what makes one moment feel complete, another only partially so?

The answer is simple. It is a phenomenon called cultural construct. We, as listeners, have become accustomed to accepting certain processes as "the way things are done" in music. Certainly, there can be deviations, but there is always a musical context within which these departures—however radical—take place, against which they are compared and judged, and to which they will always seem somewhat alien. With respect to chord progressions, that context, in a word, is Bach.

Johann Sebastian Bach (1685-1750) was an extraordinarily prolific composer. His output was enormous and his influence on European music absolutely tremendous, albeit posthumous. The popularity of his music corresponded with an age of great expansion and conquest on the part of the European nations whose musical culture he so greatly influenced.

Consequently, the systematic approach to music by Bach and his contemporaries (such as George Frideric Handel, whose works were of a comparable style and popularity), formed a standard for Western music that continues to be a factor today. The three-chord harmonic progressions of blues and rock music that sound so inevitable to a modern listener or performer would please Bach, as well—in a very real sense, he "invented" them.

The following examples are in the key of *C*-major (many chords are inverted for smooth pitch progression):

AUTHENTIC CADENCE
(aka FULL, PERFECT, COMPLETE CADENCE):
Moving from the dominant, or V chord (the triad constructed from the fifth degree of a given scale), to the tonic, or I.

AUDIO SAMPLE 54

AUTHENTIC CADENCE

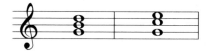

V TO I
G TO *C*

PLAGAL CADENCE:
Moving from the subdominant, or IV chord, to the tonic, or I.

AUDIO SAMPLE 55

PLAGAL CADENCE

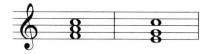

IV to I
F to *C*

IMPERFECT CADENCE (aka HALF CADENCE):
Moving from the tonic (I) to either the subdominant (IV) or the dominant (V).

AUDIO SAMPLE 56

IMPERFECT CADENCE

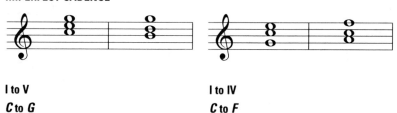

I to V   I to IV
C to *G*   *C* to *F*

DECEPTIVE CADENCE (aka INTERRUPTED CADENCE):
Moving from the dominant (V) to a chord other than the tonic (I).

AUDIO SAMPLE 57

DECEPTIVE CADENCE

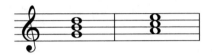

V to vi
G to *Am*

PHRYGIAN CADENCE:
Before a key change, moving from the dominant (V) or subdominant (IV) to the dominant of the key to follow, setting up a modulation to a new key.

AUDIO SAMPLE 58

PHRYGIAN CADENCE

V to VI   **NEW KEY**
G to *A*-MAJOR   *D*-MAJOR

AUDIO SAMPLE 59

PHRYGIAN CADENCE—ALTERNATE VERSION

IV to VI   **NEW KEY**
F to *A*-MAJOR   *D*-MAJOR

Chapter Twelve

(all examples are based on a root of *C*)

SYMBOL	MEANING	COMPONENTS	ROOT POSITION NOTATION
C	THE MAJOR TRIAD	*C-E-G* 1-3-5	
*C*⁶	*C*-SIXTH	*C-E-G-A* 1-3-5-6	
*C*⁶ᐟ⁹	*C*-SIX/NINE	*D-E-G-A-D* 1-3-5-6-9	
C⁽ᴬᴰᴰ⁹⁾	*C*-ADDED NINTH	*C-E-G-D* 1-3-5-9	
*CMA*⁷ (*CMAJ*⁷)	*C*-MAJOR SEVENTH	*C-E-G-B* 1-3-5-7	
*CMA*⁹ (*CMAJ*⁹)	*C*-MAJOR NINTH	*C-E-G-B-D* 1-3-5-7-9	
*CMA*¹³ *CMAJ*¹³	*C*-MAJOR THIRTEENTH	*C-E-G-B-D-A* 1-3-5-7-9-13	
*C*⁷	*C*-SEVENTH	*C-E-G-Bb* 1-3-5-*b*7	
*C*⁹	*C*-NINTH	*C-E-G-Bb-D* 1-3-5-*b*7-9	
*C*¹³	*C*-THIRTEENTH	*C-E-G-Bb-D-A* 1-3-5-*b*7-9-13	
*C*mi (*C*m)	*C*-MINOR	*C-Eb-G* 1-*b*3-5	
*C*mi⁶ (*C*m⁶)	*C*-MINOR SIXTH	*C-Eb-G-A* 1-*b*3-5-6	
*C*mi⁶ᐟ⁹	*C*-MINOR SIX/NINE	*C-Eb-G-A-D* 1-*b*3-5-6-9	

Cmi(ADD9)	C-MINOR ADDED NINTH	1-b3-5-9	
Cmi7	C-MINOR SEVENTH	C-Eb-G-Bb 1-b3-5-b7	
Cmi9	C-MINOR NINTH	C-Eb-G-Bb-D 1-b3-5-b7-9	
Cmi11	C-MINOR ELEVENTH	C-Eb-G-Bb-D-F	
Cmi13 (Cm13)	C-MINOR THIRTEENTH	C-Eb-G-Bb-D-F-A 1-b3-5-b7-9-11-13	
Cmi(MA7)	C-MINOR, MAJOR SEVENTH	C-Eb-G-B 1-b3-5-7	
Cmi7(b5)	C-MINOR SEVENTH, FLAT FIFTH (ALTERED CHORD)	C-Eb-Gb-Bb 1-b3-b5-b7	
Cdim (C0)	C-DIMINISHED	C-Eb-Gb 1-b3-b5	
C07	C-DIMINISHED SEVENTH	C-Eb-Gb-Bbb (A) 1-b3-b5-bb7 (6)	
CAUG (C+)	C-AUGMENTED	C-E-G# 1-3-#5	
Csus	C-SUSPENDED	C-F-G 1-#3 (4)-5	
C7(b5)	C-SEVENTH, FLAT FIFTH (ALTERED CHORD)	C-E-Gb-Bb 1-3-b5-b7	
C7(#5)	C-SEVENTH, SHARP FIFTH	C-E-G#-Bb 1-3-#4-b7	
C/E	C, WITH E BASS (1st INVERSION)	E-G-C 3-5-8 (1)	

Cmi⁷/F	C-MINOR SEVENTH WITH F BASS	F-C-Eb-G-Bb 4-1-b3-5-b7	
N.C.	NO CHORD		

CHORD CONSTRUCTION AND ANALYSIS

The above table supplies sufficient data for constructing and analyzing common chords. To construct chords based on tones other than C, substitute the new tonic note and follow the intervallic steps indicated.

For example:

Cmi / C minor

C-Eb-G or **1-b3-5** (of the **C** scale)

Fmi / F minor

F-Ab-C or **1-b3-5** (of the F scale)

This process is called transposition. An understanding of scale intervals is required (See CHAPTER 10).

Essentials of Music for Audio Professionals

Notate the following chords in root position, as indicated (answers are in Chapter 13):

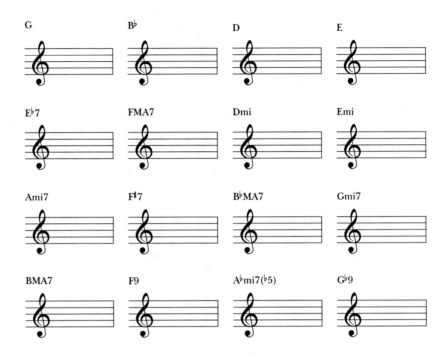

THE CHORD ARPEGGIO

A practical method for recognizing chords by ear is to hear them played as arpeggios; i.e., with each component tone played sequentially.

AUDIO SAMPLE 60

This technique is especially helpful in recognizing complex harmonies.

AUDIO SAMPLE 61

Broadly defined, a chord progression is a sequence of harmonic changes supporting a melody.

A chord progression, in itself, is not a song, although musicians can often recognize a popular work by its chord structure alone. One reason for this is that the chords usually contain most of the melody notes; in fact, many contemporary tunes are composed "chords first," the harmony suggesting the melody.

Whether the melody or harmony is composed first, the sequential progression of the harmony is intimately related to the linear progress of the melody.

In commercial recording situations, musicians are often given lead sheets, sheet music that shows the melody line with chord symbols written above it. This allows the players some performance latitude within the framework of the piece and is especially common where improvisation is called for.

In contemporary music, an arrangement usually includes chord symbols if a guitar or piano is used. In the event chord symbols are not used—in most orchestral music, for example— the harmonic progressions can be worked out by analyzing the intervallic relationships among the various parts.

The harmonic progression for Johann Pachelbel's well known *Canon in D* is revealed in the first two measures by the cello and the cembalo.

In this example the harmony changes with each quarter note and the cello plays the root of each chord. This eight-chord progression repeats for the duration of the piece.

Notice that the progression begins with *D*-major (the tonic I chord) and ends with A^7 (the dominant V).

Consider Stephen Foster's "Camptown Races":

Camptown Races — STEPHEN FOSTER

AUDIO SAMPLE 62

"Camptown Races" (Foster) David Ladd, flute.

This I-V (tonic-dominant) progression is very common, especially in folk music.

AUDIO SAMPLE 63

I-IV-V PROGRESSION

The I-IV-V (tonic-subdominant-dominant) progression is probably the single most often used harmonic sequence in Western music. Examples of this progression or its common variant, I-vi-IV-V, can be found in the works of Bach, Beethoven, and Buddy Holly.

Tchaikovsky's use of I-vi-IV-V in the ballet *The Nutcracker* predates the hundreds of rock tunes written over that progression.

AUDIO SAMPLE 64

I-vi-IV-V PROGRESSION

Here is Tchaikovsky's progression, in the key of *C*.

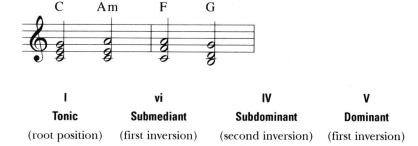

I	vi	IV	V
Tonic	**Submediant**	**Subdominant**	**Dominant**
(root position)	(first inversion)	(second inversion)	(first inversion)

Notice that *C* is a common tone to each of the first three chords. Chords with common tones make for smooth progressions.

STANDARD BLUES PROGRESSION

Harmonically, the blues form is built around the **I-IV-V** progression. The standard twelve-bar blues follows this plan:

I	**IV⁷**	**I**	**I⁷**
IV⁷	**IV⁷**	**I**	**I⁷**
V⁷	**IV⁷**	**I**	**V⁷**

AUDIO SAMPLE 65

F-BLUES PROGRESSION

Below is a chord chart for a "Blues in F"

1]	***F***	***Bb⁷***	***F***	***F⁷***
5]	***Bb⁷***	***Bb⁷***	***F***	***F⁷***
9]	***C⁷***	***Bb⁷***	***F***	***C⁷***

Again, common tones link these chord changes. *F* is common to the *F* and *Bb* chords, and *Bb* also appears in the *C⁷*.

Ostensibly unrelated harmonies can be juxtaposed for the unusual effect they produce. The second movement of Antonin Dvorák's Symphony No. 9 ("From the New World") begins with a most unusual harmonic sequence, moving from a tonal center of *E* to the key of *Db*:

E	**Bb**	**E**	**Db**	**A**	**B**	**Db**

AUDIO SAMPLE 66

Symphony No. 9, second movement (Dvorák) chord progression

The shift from *E*-natural to *Bb* is an interval of an augmented fourth, the "tritone,"—the "Diabolus in Musica," banned from the Church modes. It must have sounded quite exotic to 1893 audiences. It is speculated that Dvorák was suggesting the non-European origins of Native American and African American music.

TWO-CHORD PROGRESSIONS

The montuno is a harmonic form common in Afro-Cuban and similar music styles, used as a basis for improvisation.

A two-chord pattern is set up, usually based on I-V or I-IV, over which a soloist "ad libs" for a specified number of measures or until a cue is given.

The example follows this pattern:

Gmi   D⁷   D⁷   Gmi

AUDIO SAMPLE 67

MONTUNO PROGRESSION

HARMONIZING MELODIES

Virtually any melody in a given major key can be harmonized utilizing the tonic (I), subdominant (IV), and dominant (V) triads.

In the key of *C*, these are:

TONIC (I)
C-TRIAD

C—E—G

COMMON
TONES

SUBDOMINANT (IV)
F-TRIAD

F—A—C

DOMINANT (V)
G TRIAD

G—B—D

All the tones of the diatonic C-major scale reside within these three triads. Note the common tones.

Apply the following system to the exercise below:

I = the *C*-triad = the tonic chord (*C-E-G*)
IV = the *F*-triad = the subdominant chord (*F-A-C*)
V = the *G*-triad = the dominant chord (*G-B-D*)

Exercise # ▶ **12.6**

Analyze the following melodic fragments and choose the most appropriate chord to harmonize each measure, based on inclusion of melodic pitches in the harmony. Use Roman numerals and capital letters (answers are in Chapter 13).

EXAMPLE:

1.

SOLUTION: *Measure [1] is comprised of a C (dotted half note) and a G (quarter note), both of which appear in the C triad. Therefore, C, the I chord, is the best choice. Similar logic dictates chord selection for the remaining measures.*

2.

3.

4.

5.

Exercise # ▶ **12.7**

Analyze the following examples and identify the chords by letter name. All are written in root position (answers are in Chapter 13).

EXAMPLE:

*F*MA⁷

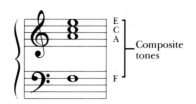

1. ___

2. ___

3. ___

4. ___

5. ___

6. ___

7. ___

8. _____

TABLATURE

In addition to identifying chords by letter names, lead sheets often use a visual representation of the guitar fret-board, known as a tablature, which shows finger positions on the strings. Horizontal lines represent the guitar frets, while the six vertical lines are the strings. Black dots indicate finger positions and white dots, or "o's," show the "open" strings.

Usually only the simplest fingerings are shown. These fingerings are often incomplete in that not all six strings are sounded. If there is neither a black dot or an "o" marking a particular string, it is not to be plucked or strummed, in most cases. (Some inconsistencies in this system appear occasionally.)

The example below shows a typical guitar tablature.

E

CHAPTER 13

Summary and Self-Evaluation

A BRIEF SUMMARY

Learning is a process, not a product: it is necessarily open-ended and on-going. This book is intended to aid the process; nothing more, nothing less. If one priority can be isolated for the audio/video professional's musical education, it is a working knowledge of musical terminology.

Performers, producers, and engineers have related concerns, but frequently divergent areas of emphasis. It is important to realize that all art exists in a continuum whose pace may accelerate or slow, whose direction may shift suddenly, even radically, while all the time remaining connected. Art conforms to or challenges established convention, but it is the continuum of convention that provides the context. Convention is nothing more than common practice, and this book is an introduction to some practices common in music, likely to be encountered by an audio/video professional.

These terms and concepts require reinforcement through practice and repetition. Use the musical vocabulary: Speak the language with peers and colleagues; make it your own through familiarity. All musical experiences, live and recorded, offer opportunities to recognize, analyze, and conceptualize the events on the intellectual plane. You now have some of the requisite data to do so.

SELF-EVALUATION

For any professional, the true self-evaluation takes place "on the job," in assessing one's success at navigating situations on a day-to-day basis. Not every eventuality can be anticipated, but the process of problem-solving is enhanced by refining skills. The exercises appearing throughout this book are intended to provide practice in these basic musical skills. The following are solutions to these exercises. Some of the exercises have precise answers; for those exercises which may have a number of correct solutions, samples are presented.

Exercise # ▶ 10.2

F whole tone scale

D♭ whole tone scale

E whole tone scale

G blues scale

F blues scale

B♭ blues scale

D blues scale

E blues scale

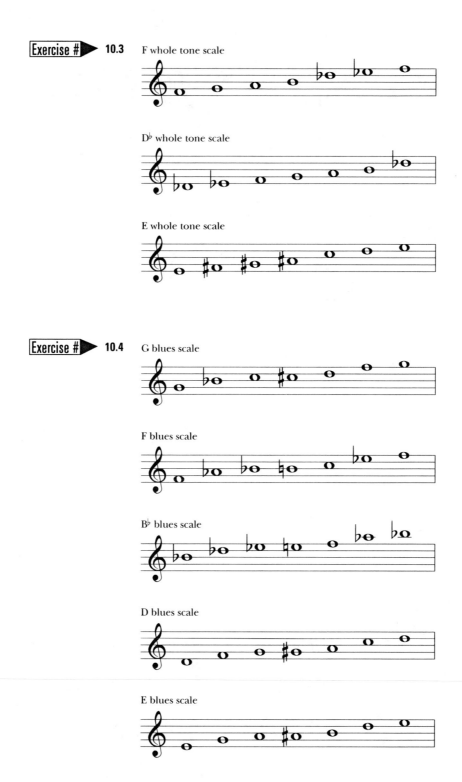

F pentatonic scale

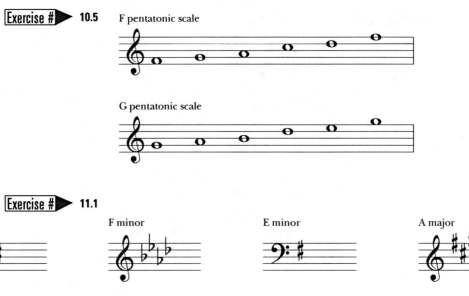

G pentatonic scale

Exercise #▶ 11.1

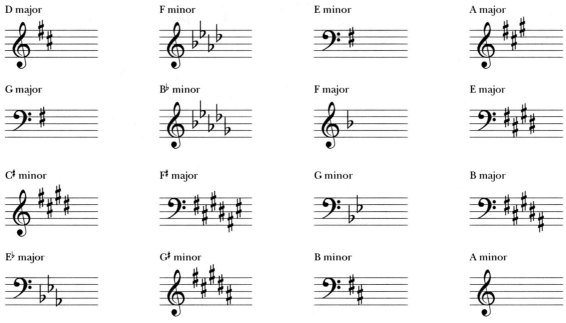

Exercise #▶ 11.2

D-MAJOR	*G*-MINOR	*D*-MINOR	*Eb*-MAJOR
*C#*MINOR	*G*-MAJOR	*A*-MINOR	*F#*MINOR
Ab-MAJOR	*C*-MAJOR	*F*-MINOR	*G#*-MINOR

TRIAD	TONES		
Eb-MAJOR TRIAD	*Eb* 1	*G* 3	*Bb* 5
G-MAJOR TRIAD	*G* 1	*B* 3	*D* 5
C#-MAJOR TRIAD	*C#* 1	*F* 3	*G#* 5
B-MAJOR TRIAD	*B* 1	*D#* 3	*F#* 5
E-MAJOR TRIAD	*E* 1	*G#* 3	*B* 5
Ab-MAJOR TRIAD	*Ab* 1	*C* 3	*Eb* 5

Exercise #▶ 12.2

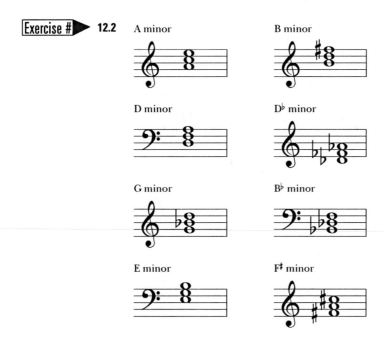

A minor   B minor

D minor   D♭ minor

G minor   B♭ minor

E minor   F♯ minor

Exercise # ▶ **12.3**

D diminished   F diminished

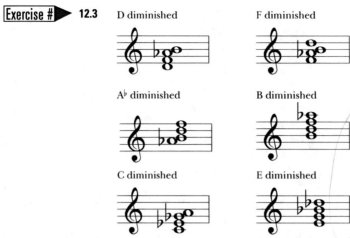

A♭ diminished   B diminished

C diminished   E diminished

Exercise # ▶ **12.4**

D augmented

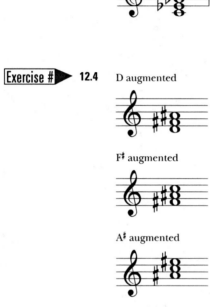

F♯ augmented

A♯ augmented

Exercise # ▶ 12.5

Exercise # ▶ 12.6

Essentials of Music for Audio Professionals

1   DMAJ^7
2   DbMAJ^7
3   B^7
4   A^7
5   Gmi^9
6   EbMA^7
7   G^{dim7}
8   D^9

Essentials of Music for Audio/Video Professionals

CHAPTER 14

Suggested Further Reading

The following is a recommended reading list and resource guide for further study and skills enhancement. All titles are in print as of this writing.

REFERENCE

Alpel, Willi. *Harvard Dictionary of Music.* Cambridge, MA: Belknap Press of Harvard University Press, 1969.

Hindley, Geoffrey, ed. *The Larousse Encyclopedia of Music.* Smithmark, 1997.

Sadie, Stanley, ed. *The New Grove Dictionary of Music and Musicians.* Washington, D.C.: Grove's Dictionaries of Music, 1981.

Slonimsky, Nicolas. *Baker's Dictionary of Music.* Edited by Richard Kassel. New York: Schirmer Books, 1997

Slonimsky, Nicolas. *Lectionary of Music.* McGraw-Hill, 1989.

Wadhams, Wayne. *Dictionary of Music Production and Engineering Terminology.* New York: Schirmer Books, 1988.

THEORY/PRACTICE

Feldstein, Sandy. *Practical Theory Complete; A Self-Instruction Music Theory Course.* Van Nuys, CA: Alfred Publishing, 1982.

Nelson, Robert and Christensen, Carl. *Foundations of Music: A Computer-Assisted Introduction.* Belmont, CA: Wadsworth, 1999.

Musical/Technical Glossary

A

A	The sixth step of the diatonic (seven-tone) ***C*-MAJOR SCALE**. The tuning pitch for orchestras is *a'* above middle *C*. Its frequency is 440 hertz (cycles per second).
ABSOLUTE MUSIC	Instrumental music generally without implications that are non-musical, i.e. words, a suggested program.
ABSOLUTE PITCH	aka **PERFECT PITCH**. The ability to distinguish the pitch of a note by ear.
A CAPPELLA	(It.) Literally "in chapel." Music for voices alone, without instrumental accompaniment.
ACCELERANDO	(It.) "Accelerate." Indication to increase tempo.
ACCENT	To emphasize a beat or note.
ACCIDENTALS	Signs indicating a change in pitch of a note: **FLAT** ♭ = lower following pitch by a half-step. **SHARP** ♯ = raise following pitch by a half-step. **NATURAL** ♮ = cancel previous sharp or flat. **DOUBLE FLAT** ♭♭ = lower following pitch by 1 full step. **DOUBLE SHARP** × = raise following pitch by 1 full step.
ACCOMPANIMENT	Any musical support of the principal part or melody.
ACOUSTIC INSTRUMENT	A musical instrument that produces sound without electrical amplification.
ACOUSTICS	The science of the behavior of sound.
ACTION	An instrument's mechanism that transfers finger motions into production of sound.
ADAGIO	(It.) Slowly. Tempo between 100-110 beats per minute (approx.).

DEUX	(Fr.) Direction for two voices or instruments to play in exact unison.
AD LIB.	**AD LIBITUM** (Lat.) Direction to play freely, "at liberty."
AEOLIAN MODE	See **MODES**, Chapter 10.
AEROPHONE	(Greek) An instrument whose sound is produced by changes in air pressure.
AFUCHE	(Afro-Cuban) A rhythm instrument producing sound by the action of beads scraping the outside of a hollow cylinder or gourd.
AGITATO	(It.) An indication to play restlessly or excitedly.
AIR	A short melody with or without words.
AL, ALL., ALLA, ALLE	(It.) To the, or in the style of.
AL FINE	(It.) To the end.
ALEATORY MUSIC	Spontaneously improvised music. Randomly performed.
ALLA BREVE	"Cut time." Time signature where the half note equals one beat. Represented by the symbol ¢.
ALLARGANDO	(It.) An indication to decrease tempo (speed) while increasing volume (loudness).
ALLEGRETTO	(It.) Light, cheerful. A tempo between 160-174 beats per minute (approx.).
ALLEGRO	(It.) Quick, lively. A tempo designation between 174-188 beats per minute (approx.).
ALL' OTTAVA	(It.) At the octave. Indicates the phrase is to be played an octave from its written pitch. 8va (**OTTAVA ALTA**) indicates the octave above, while 8vb (**OTTAVA BASSA**) indicates the octave below.
AL SEGNO	(It.) To the sign (alt. **DAL SEGNO**). A direction to repeat the music from this symbol: 𝄋
ALTERATION	Raising or lowering a pitch by use of accidentals.

ALTERED CHORDS   Chords in which one or more of the pitches have been altered by accidentals.

ALTISSIMO   (It.) The highest pitches, the extreme high register of an instrument or voice.

ALTO   (It.) "High." In early music, a male counter-tenor of falsetto voice. Now refers to the lowest female voice part, as in **S.A.T.B.**:
- Female Voices:
SOPRANO
ALTO-range: f (176 Hz) to f'' (704 Hz)
- Male Voices:
TENOR
BASS

ALTO CLEF   aka *C* **CLEF**. A sign indicating the location of the pitch *c*. Fairly uncommon in popular music, but used for alto instruments like the viola in orchestral music. (See **CLEFS**.) 𝄡

ALTO FLUTE   A flute pitched in the key of *G* (rather than *C*, or concert, pitch like the standard flute, resulting in an extended lower register. Range: *G* (96 Hz) to *g'''* (1,536 Hz).

ALTO SAXOPHONE   Pitched in the key of *Eb*, has prominent role as lead and solo instrument in stage band and jazz combo music. Fairly extensive use in solo literature and film sound track. Range: *db* (136 Hz) to *ab''* (824 Hz).

AMPLITUDE   In recording, the strength of a signal. In music, the width of a string's oscillation when set to vibrating by plucking, striking, bowing, or other method. High pitches have narrow oscillations (amplitudes), lower strings vibrate with wider relative amplitude, producing lower pitches and generating greater sound energy (db spl), hence greater signal amplitude, in the recording sense.

ANACRUSIS   A pickup note or upbeat. A rhythmic anticipation.

ANDANTE   (It.) "Walking." A tempo between 120-140 beats per minute (approx.).

ANDANTINO   (It.) Faster than andante: 140-158 beats per minute (approx.).

ANIMA, CON   (It.) "With life," literally "with soul." Animated. Also **ANIMATO**.

ANTICIPATION   Note or chord played just before a downbeat. A rhythmic, harmonic, or melodic "set-up." See **ANACRUSIS**.

ANTIPHONY (Greek/Latin) Music comprising statement and response between instruments or voices. Sequential dialogue in musical form.

APOLLO (Greek) Mythological god of music, among other things.

APPASSIONATO (It.) Passionately, with much feeling.

APPOGGIATURA (It.) From "appoggiare," to "lean on or against." An embellishment note that "leans on" or leads into the melody note. A long grace note imparting yearning, tenderness, or sorrow. Written without a slash, this note is held for a definite value (as distinguished from **ACCIACCATURA**, which is quite short and is written with a slash: ♪♪

ARABESQUE Ornamented or highly embellished music. A reference to the ornamentation in Moorish architecture.

ARCO (It.) Indication to play a stringed instrument with the bow. Also, **ARCATO**. Opposite of **PIZZICATO**—"plucked."

ARIA (It.) A song, air, melody sung by a single featured voice, with or without accompaniment. Developed in **OPERA** to showcase a strong-voiced character part.

ARPA (It.) Harp.

ARPEGGIO Playing the notes of a chord sequentially, as a harp would.

ARTICULATION The method of enunciating the individual notes of a musical piece. There are numerous types of articulation.

ASSAI (It.) Extremely, to a great extent or degree. As in **ALLEGRO ASSAI**— very fast.

A TEMPO The indication to return immediately to the original tempo after a change.

ATONAL Having no definite tonal center or key.

ATTACCA (It.) A direction to begin suddenly ("attack") a subsequent section or movement without a pause.

ATTACK The initial part of the articulation of a note; also, the beginning a musical phrase.

AUGMENTATION	With respect to rhythm, lengthening the note values of a phrase or segment.
AUGMENTED CHORD	One in which the fifth is raised by one half-step.
AUGMENTED INTERVAL	One which is larger by a half-step than major or perfect intervals.
AUTHENTIC CADENCE	A chord progression from the V (dominant) to the I (tonic). Example: a *G* chord "resolving" to a *C* chord. (See Chapter 12.)
AUTOHARP	A stringed folk instrument with chord bars that when engaged allow only the particular notes of the selected chord to sound. Similar in sound to a **ZITHER**.
AYRE	(Eng.) Short song or melody with or without words. See alt. AIR.

B

B	The seventh step of the DIATONIC (seven-tone) **C-MAJOR SCALE**. The frequency of *b'* above middle *C* is 480 Hz. In German-style musical scoring, the capital *B* indicates *B*-flat.
BACK-BEAT	Slang term for beats 2 and 4 in a four-four measure. Often accented in jazz and rock music, usually unstressed in classical forms.
BACK-UP	Term used in popular music for background harmony vocals.
BAGATELLE	(Fr.) A short, easy composition.
BAGPIPE	An ancient instrument, possibly of Middle Eastern origin, today associated primarily with Celtic cultures. The Scotch type has drone pipes and a "chanter" on which the melody is fingered; the air bag is replenished by the breath. The Irish Uilleann pipes use a bellows system for air supply.
BALALAIKA	(Russ.) A folk guitar (available in various sizes), usually featuring three strings and played with a **PICK** or plectrum.
BALLAD	A romantic popular song, usually with words. Also, a song relating exploits of a heroine or hero in a narrative style.

BALLET (Fr.) Dance or mime set to music and containing a story line.

BAMBOULA (Creole) Barefoot dancing to banjo music developed by black dock workers in New Orleans in the 1850's.

BAND Technically, an ensemble consisting of woodwinds, brass, and percussion, as opposed to an **ORCHESTRA** which includes strings. Extended to mean any musical group other than an orchestra.

BANDONEON (Sp.) A Spanish guitar tuned a minor third lower than is customary. See **GUITAR**.

BANJO A five-string instrument with a long neck and fretboard and a circular body, with a parchment or plastic resonating membrane, played with a **PLECTRUM**. Range: *C* (128 Hz) to *e'''* (1,280 Hz).

BAR Technically, a vertical line on the staff that divides the measures. By extension, the measure itself.

BARBERSHOP Male or female quartet **A CAPELLA** singing, originating in America in the late 19th century. Melody is usually carried by the second as opposed to the top voice. Close harmonies and unexpected motion are frequent. Term derives from the music's informal origin, and style can be considered a forerunner of urban "doo-wop" vocal.

BAR LINES Vertical lines drawn on music manuscript to indicate division between measures or sections of a composition. The double bar indicates "end." Two vertical dots next to the double bar indicate sections to be repeated. See Chapters 2, 3.

BARCAROLE (It.) Originally a type of work song, usually in three-four or six-eight time, sung by Venetian gondoliers.

BARD (Welsh) A self-accompanied Celtic musician-poet who composed verses while playing the **HARP** or **LUTE**. A medieval equivalent to the African griot or the American rapper.

BARITONE Male voice range between **TENOR** (above) and **BASS** (below). Range: *G* (96 Hz) to *d'* (280 Hz).

BARITONE HORN A brass piston-valved instrument in *Bb*, covering a range from *E* (80 Hz) to *bb'* (460 Hz).

BARITONE SAXOPHONE	The **SAXOPHONE** equivalent of the **BARITONE** voice. Pitched in *Eb*. Range: *Db* (68 Hz) to *ab'* (412 Hz).
BAROQUE	Style of music, art, and architecture that was dominant in Europe from about 1600 to the death of J. S. Bach (the period's most famous composer) in 1750. Characterized by the use of rhythmic complexity, melodic **COUNTERPOINT**, and a harmonic system that continues as the basis of pop, jazz, and rhythm & blues songwriting.
BARREL HOUSE	An early 20th century New Orleans-style piano playing; post ragtime, pre jazz—showing elements of these and of the blues.
BARREL ORGAN	See **HURDY GURDY**, instrument producing tones by the cranking of a cylinder.
BASS	The lowest pitched male voice. Range: *F* (88 Hz) to *c'* (256 Hz). Also, the lowest instrumental part in a composition. Lowest frequencies in recording or sound reinforcement.
BASS CLEF	aka *F*-**CLEF**. See Chapter 4. 𝄢
BASS DRUM	The largest orchestral or marching drum, capable of the lowest frequencies produced by percussion.
BASS HORN	aka **TUBA**, lowest voice in the brass family.
BASS, STRING	aka **DOUBLE BASS** or **CONTRABASS**. The orchestral bass viol. Lowest voice in the string section. Range: *EE* (40 Hz) to *g* (198 Hz).
BASSO CONTINUO	(It.) A moving-**BASS** keyboard part originating the Baroque period and still employed in contemporary music.
BASSO OSTINATO	(It.) aka **GROUND BASS**. A repetitive **BASS** figure. Contemporary versions are "Boogie Woogie" piano or repeating rhythm & blues electric bass licks, for instance.
BASSOON	The **BASS** of the **OBOE** family, pitched two octaves below the oboe. Range: *Bb* (115 Hz) to *eb''* (608 Hz). (The **CONTRABASSOON** is pitched one octave lower.)
BASS TROMBONE	Brass instrument pitched just above the **TUBA**. Range: *C* (64 Hz) to *bb'* (460 Hz).
BATON	(Fr.) Literally, "stick." Used as a visual aid in conducting a musical ensemble.

BATTERIE (Fr.) The percussion section of an ensemble.

BATTUTA (It). Instruction to play in strict time, with accented beats. Also **ABATTUTA**.

BEAM horizontal line joining a group of notes (in place of writing individual flags). See Chapter 3.

BEAT The regular timing pulses that establish tempo.

BEAT TONES Pulsating tones (difference tones, or subharmonics) produced when two close tones are not matching in pitch (frequency). As pitches move closer to matching frequency, pulses occur less frequently until they are virtually imperceptible.

BEATS PER MINUTE aka **METRONOME MARKING**. Tempos expressed as a mathematical equation. Ex.: ♩=120 , ♩=72

BE-BOP aka **BOP**. A Jazz style of improvisation originating in the late 1930's and 40's, associated with Dizzy Gillespie, Charlie Parker, Thelonious Monk, et al. Characterized by double-time playing over extended harmonies, requiring extraordinary intellectual and technical skills. In a sense, the successor to **SWING**, which was essentially dance music.

BEL An arbitrary measure of the loudness of sound. The decibel (one tenth of a bel) is considered the smallest increment in a change of loudness perceptible to the human ear. Often capitalized in homage to audio pioneer Alexander Graham Bell.

BEL CANTO (It.) Literally, "beautiful song." An 18th-century singing style characterized by an emphasis on tone quality (timbre) and emotional tenderness.

BELL A hollow metal instrument sounded by an external hammer or internal clapper. Also, the flared end of a wind instrument.

BELL-LYRE aka **GLOCKENSPIEL**, a parade version of the **XYLOPHONE**, played with one mallet. Range: *a"* (880 Hz) to *a""* (3,520 Hz).

BELLY aka **SOUNDBOARD**. The hollow mid-section of a string instrument which resonates when the instrument is played, producing its particular tonal quality or timbre.

BEND An embellishment of a note, common for wind players but possible to some degree on most instruments. The note is sounded in tune, then "bent" **FLAT** and finally returned to true pitch, producing an approximation of African or Middle Eastern vocal stylization or animal vocalization, or even the **DOPPLER EFFECT**.

BERCEUSE (Fr.) A lullaby or cradle song.

BILAWAL SCALE (Hindi) A scale from the Indian subcontinent which is the equivalent of the European seven-tone or **DIATONIC** scale (i.e., do-re-mi-etc.). See Chapter 10.

BINARY CODE A system of rendering musical, visual, or other information in digital form for storage, transmission, or retrieval and playback: Any numerical value can be rendered as a combination of 1's or 0's to represent amplitudes and frequencies over time. This concept, originally developed for general computer data, has revolutionized audio and video production.

BINARY FORM A fundamental method for structuring musical compositions in two parts, e.g.:
melody, verse
A—B or
A—B—A
See Chapter 7.

BINAURAL Literally, "two ears." A type of **STEREO** (opposite of **MONAURAL**). Specifically, a recording technique using two microphones placed at the relative position of the ears, yielding a realistic live stereo effect when the resulting recording is played back through headphones.

BITONALITY A type of music in which two keys are employed simultaneously. For example, examine the music of Charles Ives. Also see **POLYPHONY**, also see Chapter 11.

BLOCK CHORDS Keyboard chords played simultaneously, in octaves.

BLOCK FLUTE aka **FIPPLE FLUTE**, an end-blown flute; a **RECORDER**.

BLUEGRASS A type of American country music featuring string instrumentation, especially guitar, banjo, fiddle. Usually fast and rhythmically complex, derived essentially from the English folk music tradition.

BLUE NOTE   A flattening of the pitch for dramatic effect in a jazz or blues context. Usually employed on the third and seventh (and sometimes on the fifth) steps of the scale.

BLUES   A form of American music resulting from the fusion of African melodic, rhythmic, and form concepts with European harmonic structure. See Chapters 7, 10, 12.

BOEHM SYSTEM   A system for improved keying of **FLUTE, CLARINET,** and **OBOE** fingerings developed in the 19th century by Theobald Boehm, dramatically advancing facility and intonation.

BOLERO   (Sp.) A Spanish dance, of Moroccan origin, in three-four time with a rhythmic **OSTINATO.** In contemporary Latin music the term is less specific and can refer to any relatively slow dance music.

BONES   Strips of wood or actual animal rib bones held between the fingers and used as percussion instruments.

BONGO DRUMS   In Afro-Cuban music, a tunable pair of small hand drums held between the knees and functioning as the **SOPRANO** voice in the percussion section.

BOOGIE-WOOGIE   A style of piano music featuring blues-based improvisation over an ostinato bass. See **BASSO OSTINATO.**

BOSSA NOVA   (Sp.) An Anglicized version of the Brazilian samba, introduced to the jazz idiom in the early 1960's. Characterized by a variation on the syncopated clave rhythm pattern. See **CLAVE,** also Chapter 3.

BOUCHE FERME   (Fr.) "Mouth closed," an indication for vocalists to hum.

BOURRE   (Fr.) A French and/or Spanish folk dance in a quick tempo.

BOUZOUKI   (Greek) A traditional Greek folk instrument with multiples of strings, played with a plectrum. Probably derived from the Indian **SITAR** by way of its Persian and Turkish variants.

BOW   The wood and horsehair implement for vibrating the strings of instruments of the **VIOLIN** family. Rosin applied to the hairs produces the necessary friction and the bow's tension is adjusted by a screw-operated mechanism called a **FROG.**

BRASS INSTRUMENTS Wind instruments using a cup or funnel shaped mouthpiece to focus the vibration of a player's lips, and amplifying the frequencies produced through the resonating chamber of the horn. Available frequencies result from the fundamentals and harmonics inherent in the particular length of the tubing involved.

BREAK The point in the singer's range where a change in quality or timbre occurs. Also, in the clarinet, the noticeable texture change between *Bb* (above middle *C*) and the *B* natural above. Also, a rhythmic pause at the end of a phrase which a soloist "fills." Also a short **CADENZA**, or solo.

BREVE (It.) Obsolete rhythmic notation with a value of two whole notes.

BRIDGE On a string instrument, the ridge which supports the strings and serves to impart some of their vibrations to the body of the instrument. Also, the transitional part of a popular song which sets up a return to the main melody. aka **RELEASE**.

BRIO (It.) "Spirit," hence **CON BRIO**, "with spirit."

BROKEN CHORD A chord in which notes are played sequentially as opposed to simultaneously. See **ARPEGGIO**.

BUFFA (It.) Comic, humorous, in a comic style; e.g. **OPERA BUFFA**, comic opera.

BUGLE A predecessor to the modern trumpet, without keys or valves. Today it is used primarily in military context for signalling, parade ground, campsite, or battlefield commands. The modern version, pitched in the key of *G* has a valve system allowing for much greater facility than the "natural horn." Range: *db* (136 Hz) to *c'''* (1,024 Hz).

BULL ROARER An instrument dating back to prehistoric times that comprises a thin flat wooden stick or bone fragment with a hole in one end, attached to a string. When whirled it produces a sound whose characerics are determined by the size and density of the wood, the length of string, and the speed and force employed.

BUSKER In English folk music, an instrumentalist capable of improvising.

BYZANTINE CHANT Ceremonial music of the medieval Byzantine Empire, originating about 300 a.d.

C   The first step (**TONIC**) of the **DIATONIC SCALE** of the same name. The frequency of middle *C* is 256 Hz.

CABASA   A Brazilian percussion instrument made from a gourd and handle with beads strung on the outside. See **AFUCHE**.

CACHUCHA   (Sp.) An Andalusian dance in fast triple time.

CACOPHONY   Term indicating random noise, musical chaos, or extreme dissonance.

CADENCE   A melodic and harmonic resolution or resting point. Also, the end of a chord progression or series of changes. See Chapter 12. Also, the tempo of a musical selection.

CADENZA   (It.) A solo in free time, usually at or near the end of a composition, that allows an individual player to display command of the instrument. Can be improvised or written.

CAISSE   (Fr.) The drum.

CAKEWALK   Originally, a competition dance invented by black slaves as a parody of formal European styles favored by southern aristocracy. A prize, usually a cake, was awarded for the most humorous, outrageous, or athletic dance. The antecedent of break dancing and competitive ballroom and ice dancing.

CALLIOPE   (Greek) In mythology, the muse or goddess of inspiration, responsible for eloquence and heroic poetry. Also, a steam-driven pipe organ used at circuses, fairs, and on riverboats, producing adequate **DECIBELS** to be heard over great distance. Its frequency range corresponds approximately to that of the **PIPE ORGAN**.

CALYPSO   (W. Indian) A form of popular song originating in Trinidad and Jamaica, usually as political or social satire. Melodies are short and repetitious, and lyrics are often improvised and utilize dialect speech patterns. In the cultural tradition of the African griot. One of the antecedents of hip-hop and rap.

CAMERA   (It.) A Baroque term for music to be performed in a room, rather than a concert hall or stadium venue.

C-MELODY SAXOPHONE   A saxophone sounding one step higher than the common *Bb* tenor saxophone. Essentially obsolete, but heard occasionally on recordings of 1940's swing bands as a solo instrument.

CAN CAN   A French music hall dance of the late 19th century, featuring a high-kicking female chorus line.

CANCION   (Sp.) "Song."

CANON   (Gr.) "Rule." Music written for several voices. A principal voice initiates the melody, which is then imitated exactly or in variation by successive voices. The round is a strict canon form in which each voice is an exact repeat of the previous one.

CANTABLE   (It.) A direction to perform instrumental music as if it were vocalized. "Like singing."

CANTATA   (It.) Vocal composition of several movements for one or several voices with instrumental accompaniment. Music of this type, when written for a solo instrument, is called **SONATA**.

CANTICLE   A sacred hymn or song of scriptural origin.

CANTO   (It.) A song. Also, the highest vocal part. Also, a part or division of an epic poem.

CANTOR   A singer or chanter. Also, one who sings in the synagogue.

CANTUS FIRMUS   (Latin) "Fixed Song." Melody sung in unison or the principal melody against which a **COUNTERPOINT** is set.

CAPELL-MEISTER   (Ger.) Musical director of a choir or orchestra.

CAPO, DA   (It.) "From the head." An instruction to repeat a piece of music from the beginning.

CAPRICCIO   (It.) "Caprice." A relatively brief instrumental piece in a whimsical style often including sound effects.

CARILLON   (Fr.) A set of chromatically tuned bells covering three or four octaves hung in a tower or church steeple, played by keyboard or clock-work mechanism.

CASTANETS   (Sp.) A Spanish hand percussion instrument consisting of two sets of shell-shaped clappers controlled by hand and finger motion of the player or dancer.

CASTRATO (It.) A male singer with a childhood **SOPRANO** voice. In earlier times, a boy castrated in pre-adolescence to preserve this vocal range through adulthood.

CAVATINA (It.) A short vocal or instrumental piece without repeats.

CAXAXI [*Pron: ka-shè-she*] An Afro-Brazilian hand percussion instrument, bell-shaped, made of wicker and gourd shell, filled with seeds or small stones, played in pairs and capable of multiple sounds.

CELESTA (It.) A small keyboard instrument that produces sounds when hammers strike tuned steel bars.

CELLO (It.) A contraction of **VIOLONCELLO**, the string voice in the modern orchestra between **VIOLA** and **BASS**. Range is from *C* (64 Hz) to *g'* (384 Hz).

CENT A measurement of musical intervals. Each semitone (chromatic half-step) is divided into 100 cents. A pitch 50 cents above *C*, for example, would be the quarter-tone halfway between *C* and *C*$^{\#}$. These "cent" measurements are not linear. Unlike measurements in Hz, they are fractions or "percents."

CHACONNE (Fr.) A Baroque style composition in three-four with repeated harmonies and a fixed bass part. Melodic variations are improvised within this framework.

CHALUMEAU (Fr.) The lowest-register instrument of the **CLARINET** family. It has a distinctly "wooden" or **OBOE**-like texture.

CHAMBER MUSIC Music written for a small number of players or vocalists, each performing a separate part (as opposed to orchestral music, in which many players share parts). Music to be performed in a small venue.

CHANGES Colloquial expression for harmonic sequence or chord progression within a composition.

CHANSON (Fr.) "Song" in the pop style.

CHANT (Latin) "Song." Technically, any **MONOPHONIC** (without harmony) melody which is sung by an individual or group. Almost always religious or spiritual in nature.

CHANTER The finger pipe of the **BAGPIPE**.

CHARLESTON A popular dance originating in the 1920's based on this rhythm:

CHEST VOICE The low register of the singing voice.

CHIMES An instrument of the **METALLOPHONE** family consisting of tubular bells vertically suspended, played with a hard leather hammer. Range: from c' (256 Hz) to f'' (704 Hz).

CHINESE MUSETTE A double-reed instrument with a flared brass bell, similar to the middle-eastern **SHAWM**. It is built in various keys and has a range approximating the Bb clarinet, though not fully chromatic.

CHIUSO (It.) "Close or Shut." An indication on a musical score for the **FRENCH HORN** player to alter pitch and/or tone by inserting the hand into the bell.

CHOIR A group of singers or related instruments (e.g., **BRASS CHOIR**).

CHORALES Hymns developed during the Protestant reformation that replaced **GREGORIAN CHANTS** in the new liturgy; this form was initiated by Martin Luther. By extension, any music constructed in a similar form.

CHORAL MUSIC Ensemble vocal music with multiple singers on each part.

CHORD Multiple pitches sounded simultaneously. See Chapters 8, 9, 12.

CHORDOPHONES (Greek) The family of stringed instruments, bowed, plucked, or struck.

CHORD ORGAN Small upright electronic instrument with a keyboard for playing melody and buttons for playing chords. A console version of the **ACCORDION**.

CHORD SYMBOLS A shorthand version of writing harmonies, using the alphabet and numerals rather than standard notation. See Chapter 12.

CHORUS A vocal ensemble. Mixed chorus: **SOPRANO, ALTO, TENOR, and BASS (S.A.T.B.)**.
- Women's Chorus: **SOPRANO 1, SOPRANO 2, ALTO 1, ALTO 2 (S.S.A.A.)**
- Men's Chorus: **TENOR 1, TENOR 2, BARITONE, BASS (T.T.B.B.)**

Also, the part of a popular song known as the **REFRAIN** or **HOOK**.

CHROMATIC	(Greek) "Color." Movement by consecutive half-steps (semitones). Also, using notes not belonging to a particular given key or scale.
CHROMATIC INSTRUMENT	One which is capable of producing all the notes of the chromatic scale (e.g., a **CLARINET** as opposed to a **PENNY WHISTLE**).
CHROMATIC SCALE	aka **12-TONE SCALE**. 12 successive half-steps (semitones). Ex: The 12 piano keys, black and white, from any *C* to the *B* natural above it.
CHROMATIC SIGNS	**ACCIDENTALS**; sharps, flats, and natural signs.
CHURCH MODES	aka **ECCLESIASTICAL MODES**. Eight basic scales approved by Pope Gregory I around 600 a.d. in order to standardize Christian liturgical music. Two of these, the **IONIAN** and the **AEOLIAN**, are the basis for the present **MAJOR** and **MINOR** systems. See Chapter 10.
CIMBALOM	See **DULCIMER**.
CIRCLE OF FIFTHS	A device for modulation (changing key), covering all 12 keys by progressing to consecutive keys in fifths above the previous keys.
CLARINET	A single-reed woodwind instrument invented about 1700 by J. C. Denner of Nuremburg. Generallyit is built in *Bb*, but there have been clarinets in *C*, *A*, *Eb*, and *Ab*. It is chromatic throughout its wide range which, for the *Bb* clarinet, extends from *d* (144 Hz) to *ab'''* (1,648 Hz).
CLARINO	(It.) A Baroque-era valveless **PICCOLO TRUMPET**. It could be played chromatically only in its **ALTISSIMO** (extreme upper) range. Extraordinarily difficult to play, it was rendered obsolete by the **CLARINET**. Its usable range was from *c''* (512 Hz) to *c''''* (2,048 Hz).
CLASSICAL MUSIC	Technically, European **SYMPHONIC** and **CHAMBER** music created during the Classical period, between (approximately) 1750 and 1850. Principal composers of the period include Hayden, Mozart, etc. Colloquially, term is often applied to any **ORCHESTRAL** music outside the pop or jazz idioms.

CLÁVE (Cuban) [*Pron: Clá-vay*] A hand percussion instrument composed of two hard wooden sticks, one held cupped by the palm and struck by the other. The high-frequency transients produced (above 5 kHz) are easily audible even in a large percussion ensemble. Crucial to establishing tempo and rhythm in Afro-Cuban, Brazilian, and related musics. There are strict patterns observed in authentic **SALSA** and **SAMBA**, though pop music often uses the clave texturally.

CLAVIETTA A plastic reed instrument with side keyboard attached with a range of about 2.5 octaves.

CLAVICHORD A keyboard instrument invented in the 13th century, popular through the 17th. Made obsolete by the **PIANOFORTE**. Later models had a compass of *FF* (44 Hz) to *f'''* (1,408 Hz) and were touch-sensitive for volume and vibrato.

CLAVIER (Fr.) Technically, any keyboard instrument with strings; as opposed to ORGAN PIPES, for instance.

CLEF A symbol in music notation designating a particular line or space on the staff as a particular pitch. See Chapter 4.

CLICK TRACK A cue pulse, pre-recorded on tape or film or produced by a metronome in real time and sent to conductor and/or performers through a headset to establish a strict tempo and/or synchronize sound to film or video.

CLOSE HARMONY Chords voiced with their constituent pitches close together as opposed to "open." See Chapter 12.

CODA (It.) "Tail." The tag or ending of a musical selection.

COL, COLL', COLLA (Ital). "With the" (e.g., **COL ARCO**: with the bow; **COL TRUMPETS**: with the trumpets).

COLOR Musical slang for altering a note, phrase, or instrumental texture by means of muting or other devices that change the frequency recipe. A more precise term is **TIMBRE** [*pron: tám-ber*].

COLORATURA (It.) Ornaments or embellishments in vocal music, especially as related to the **SOPRANO** voice.

COMMA In musical notation, an indication to a vocalist or wind player to take a breath.

COMMON TIME Four-four meter. Sometimes indicated by a capital C, which historically was not a "C" at all, but a broken circle; used in the Middle Ages and called the **IMPERFECTUM**. See Chapter 3.

COMPASS The frequency range of a voice or instrument from its lowest to highest possibilities. Usually expressed on the staff or by letter names rather than in hertz. See **FREQUENCY TEMPLATE** in Chapter 4.

COMPOSITION Original music. Also the act of writing same (as opposed to **ARRANGING**).

COMPOUND INTERVALS Those which exceed a one-octave range.

COMPOUND TIME Technically, any meter including or exceeding six parts per measure and containing at least two principal accents (e.g., six-four, six-eight, nine-four, nine-eight). See Chapter 3.

CON (It.) "With" (e.g., **CON ANIMATO**: "with spirit").

CONCERT Music performed for an audience. Also, "together," "in accord."

CONCERT GRAND The largest **GRAND PIANO**.

CONCERTINA A small hexagonal **ACCORDION** with a button keyboard. Invented in 1829 by Sir Charles Wheatstone. Its range is *g* (192 Hz) to *g''''* (1,536 Hz).

CONCERT MASTER From (Ger.) **KONCERTMEISTER**. The lead violinist of an orchestra and/or the assistant conductor.

CONCERTO (It.) A showcase piece for an instrumental soloist (or small group) with full orchestral accompaniment.

CONCERTO GROSSO (It.) A Baroque form of **CONCERTO** for small group (**CONCERTINO**) alternating with an orchestra (**CONCERTO GROSSO**).

CONCERT PITCH An international standard of tuning. Modern agreement sets *A* above middle *C*, (*a'*) as 440 Hz, or cycles per second. See Chapter 4.

CONCORD A relative term implying harmonious agreement of pitch. The opposite of **DISCORD**. (Note: The octave is not divided uniformly in all musical traditions. Music that sounds discordant to a European can be quite harmonious in Indonesia, for example.)

CONDENSED SCORE An orchestral score wherein all parts are condensed onto two staves for easy scanning by the conductor. Used primarily for study reference.

CONGA An Americanized version of a popular Cuban dance of the 1930's, featuring dancers in column. Three forward steps are followed by a unison kick on the syncopated beat:

(kick)

CONGAS [*Pron: Koón-gas*] Afro-Cuban drums usually played in sets of three of graduating sizes, by hand. Made of wood, they are cylindrical in shape, about 36 inches in height, open at the bottom with a skin top head. Capable of producing multiple timbres and pitches, these drums are integral to all African and Latin musics and are widely used in pop music.

CONSOLE (Fr.) The keyboard, pedal, and stops apparatus of the **ORGAN**. Also, the main audio or video mixing desk containing the engineer's or editor's control panel.

CONSONANCE The result of **HARMONY** that is "pleasing to the ear." A subjective judgement. (See **CONCORD**.) Opposite of **DISSONANCE**.

CONSORT A **CHAMBER** ensemble in 16th and 17th century England composed of similar instruments (e.g., a **FLUTE** consort).

CONTRA (It.) "Under," "Low."

CONTRABASS The **DOUBLE BASS**, lowest pitched of the orchestral string family. Range: *EE* (40 Hz) to *g'* (384 Hz).

CONTRABASSOON Lowest pitched of the woodwinds. Range: *BBb* (58 Hz) to *cb'* (300 Hz).

CONTRALTO (It.) Lowest of the female voice divisions. Range: *f* (176 Hz) to *d"* (576 Hz).

CONTRAPUNTAL See **COUNTERPOINT**.

CONTRARY MOTION Melodic lines or parts parts moving in opposite directions.

COR (Fr.) "Horn." When used alone, refers to the **FRENCH HORN**.

COR ANGLAIS	(Fr.) The **ENGLISH HORN**. Actually, a corruption of **COR ANGLE**, referring to an 18th-century **ALTO OBOE** built in the key of *F*, which had an angled mouthpipe and bell. A double reed instrument of the woodwind family, the modern version of which has an oboe-type mouthpiece and a bulb-shaped bell. Range: *e* (160 Hz) to *a"* (880 Hz).
CORDA	(It.) "String;" e.g., **CORDA VUOTA**: "Open (unstopped) string." **UNA CORDA**: "One string." Use soft pedal on piano. **DUE CORDA**: "Two strings." Play the same note on two strings to increase volume (a doubling of in-phase oscillations—violin, etc.). **TRE CORDA**: "Three strings." Release the soft pedal on piano, allowing all strings to resonate. Also **TUTTI LE CORDA**.
CORNET	A relative of the **TRUMPET** with the same range (*e* [160 Hz] to *c'''* [1,024 Hz]) but a somewhat different timbre, due primarily to the diameter of the mouthpipe and the wrap of the tubing.
CORNETT	See **ZINKE**.
CORNO	(It.) "Horn." Specifically, the curved valveless natural or **HUNTING HORN**, the ancestor of the modern **FRENCH HORN**.
CORONA	(It.) "Crown." Refers to the **FERMATA**, ⌒, a symbol indicating a sustaining of the note.
COUNJAILLE	(Creole) Another name for the **BAMBOULA**.
COUNTERPOINT	The superimposing of two or more melodies to produce harmonic and rhythmic combinations. A further evolution of Medieval **POLYPHONY**. Strict rules for counterpoint were developed by Johann Fux [pron: "fooks"] about 1725. J. S. Bach (d. 1750) is considered master of the technique.
COUNTER TENOR	The highest male voice, sung in **FALSETTO**. Corresponds to the high lead vocals in rock or doo-wop music.
COUNTRY DANCE	16th-century popular English folk dance.
COUNTRY MUSIC	American folk-style music with its origins in traditional English songs brought over by settlers in the 17th century. Variations include bluegrass, hillbilly, and others. Modern hybrid forms are country pop, southern rock, country western, western swing, etc., but such terms tend to be of marketing, rather than musical origin.

CRESCENDO (It.) A direction to increase dynamic level over time. Opposite of **DECRESCENDO**. See Chapter 5.

CROOK Curved metal mouthpipe of some woodwind instruments. Also, curved metal-tube inserts for brass instruments which have the effect of shortening or lengthening the resonating chamber, thereby raising or lowering the inherent frequencies.

CROTCHET (Fr.) In the British system, the name for the quarter note. See Chapter 3.

CROSS RHYTHM Two different rhythm patterns played simultaneously, e.g.,

CRWTH (Welsh) [pron. "kruth"] A Celtic instrument of the Middle Ages thought to be an ancestor of the modern **VIOLIN**, with six strings tuned in octaves, played by bowing.

CUE A signal between conductor and ensemble, or among a group of musicians, while playing.

CUE MIX The headphone mix in a recording session.

CUE NOTES Small annotations on an individual part indicating musical cues performed by another player or section.

CYMBALS **GONG**-like percussion instruments probably originating in the Middle East, made from thin brass alloy, designed to be struck together or by means of a stick or mallet. Depending on size, density, and playing technique, the dynamic and frequency ranges are extraordinary and resulting textures remarkably complex.

CYMBALOM See **DULCIMER**.

CZARDAS Hungarian Dance form in two movements, slow (**LASSU**), then fast two-four (**FRISS**), often containing an extended **ACCELERANDO**.

D

D The second step of the diatonic **C-MAJOR SCALE**. The frequency of *d* above middle *C* is 280 Hz.

DA	(It.) "From," "by."
DA CAPO	(It.) Repeat from the head (beginning). Abbr. to **D.C.**
DAL SEGNO	(It.) Repeat "from the sign": 𝄋 Abbr. to **D.S.**
DAMPER	A pedal mechanism to dampen or stop string or keyboard vibrations.
DECEPTIVE CADENCE	aka **INTERRUPTED CADENCE**. Moving from the **DOMINANT** to a chord other than the **TONIC**. See Chapter 12.
DECIBEL	One tenth of a bel, abbreviated **dB**. A logarithmic measurement of sound level (or electrical energy). When referenced to sound pressure, 1 dB represents the smallest perceptible increment.
DECRESCENDO	(It.) A decrease in volume over time. Opposite of **CRESCENDO**.
DEMISEMIQUAVER	In British musical parlance, a 32nd note. See Chapter 3.
DESCANT	The **TENOR** or **TREBLE** voice or vocal part. Derived from the Latin **DISCANTUS**, an early form of harmony featuring a kind of **COUNTERPOINT** sung above the original melody.
DETACHE	(Fr.) "Detached." Instruction for string players to separate the notes in a passage.
DEVELOPMENT	Usually the second section of a musical work (**SYMPHONY, SONATA,** etc.) in which the original theme is explored and altered rhythmically, melodically, and/or harmonically.
DIABOLUS (IN MUSICA)	(Latin) "Satan in the music." A Medieval description of the interval of the **AUGMENTED FOURTH** (**DIMINISHED FIFTH**), aka **TRITONE**. Under Gregorian (Church mode) rules of composition, it was scrupulously avoided. See Chapter 10.
DIATONIC SCALE	(Greek) "Seven—tone." The familiar *do-re-me,* etc. major scale of European music. See Chapter 10.
DIDJEREDOO	Australian aboriginal wind instrument, made out of a long (five feet or more), hollowed-out tree trunk of small diameter (three inches or so). Played like a natural horn, usually with a circular breathing technique. Produces a fundamental pitch in the approximate **BASS** or **BARITONE** register (60 Hz to 280 Hz), as well as harmonics, dependent on the skill and technique of the player.

DIMINISHED CHORD   A chord in which the third and fifth are lowered by a half step. See Chapter 12.

DIMINUENDO   (It.) aka **DECRESCENDO**. A diminishing of volume over time. Opposite of **CRESCENDO**. ⸻⸺

DIMINUTION   The reduction of the note values of a musical passage by one-half.

DISCORD   Opposite of **CONCORD**. A subjective term.

DISSONANCE   Opposite of **CONSONANCE**, and an equally subjective judgement.

DIVERTIMENTO   (It.) Instrumental composition made up of four or more short movements, with a light-hearted style.

DIVERTISSEMENT   (Fr.) A **DIVERTIMENTO**, often performed as intermission music.

DIVISI   (It.) Abbreviated to **DIV**. To divide performers equally on two or more parts, within a single orchestral part.

DOIT   A direction to brass players to imitate the sound of this word by attacking a note and abruptly sliding up, ending in a clipped manner.

DOLCE   (It.) "Sweet." Indication to play sweetly.

DOMINANT CHORD   One whose root is a fifth above the **TONIC**. See Chapter 12.

DOMINANT INTERVAL   The fifth degree of the **DIATONIC SCALE**. See Chapter 12.

DOPPEL   (Ger.) "Double."

DOPPLER EFFECT   The apparent shift in observed frequency when the source or observer is in motion.

DORIAN MODE   See Chapter 10.

DOT   In musical notation, there are several meanings, depending on location. Placed after a note, it increases the note's value by one half. A second dot adds one half the value of the first dot. Placed above or below a note, it is an indication to play **STACCATO**. Two vertical dots next to a double bar indicate a **REPEAT**. See Chapter 3.

DOUBLE BAR   Two vertical lines delineating a section or end of a composition.

DOUBLE BASS	Any instrument which sounds an octave lower than written. aka **CONTRABASS**.
DOUBLE *Bb* BASS	The **SOUSAPHONE** or **HELICON**.
DOUBLE FLAT	♭♭ Lowers the following note by one whole step.
DOUBLE REED	Any instrument that produces sound by air flow vibrating two reeds; e.g., **OBOE**.
DOUBLE SHARP	× Raises the following note by one whole step.
DOUBLE STOP	Playing two strings at a time, either in unison, octaves, or harmony.
DOUBLE TIME	Direction to play twice as fast.
DOWN BEAT	The initial beat of a piece of music. The direction to begin.
DRONE	A continuous, unbroken note or cluster of notes.
DUET	A piece of music for two performers.
DULCIMER	A stringed instrument played with small hammers, its metal strings above a wood sound box. Of Middle Eastern orgin (the Santur). The **CYMBALOM** is a variant. Also, the Appalachian folk instrument which has three strings and is plucked. Frequency ranges of both instruments correspond roughly to the acoustic **GUITAR** and **MANDOLIN**, respectively. Ranges: **HAMMER DULCIMER**—*E* (80 Hz) to *a"* (880 Hz). **APPALACHIAN** (plucked)—*g* (198 Hz) to *a'''* (1,760 Hz).
DUODECAPHONIC	(Greek) Twelve-tone music. Music utilizing the **CHROMATIC** (twelve-tone) scale.
DUPLE METER	Any time signature divisible by two. See Chapter 3.
DUPLETS	Two notes, written with a bracket above, played evenly in the space of three. See Chapter 3.
DYNAMIC MARKS	Notation symbols indicating levels of musical volume, amplitude, or changes in same over time. These variations create the illusion of space or distance. See Chapter 5.

Essentials of Music for Audio Professionals

E The third step of the **C-MAJOR SCALE**. The frequency of *e'* above middle *C* is 320 Hz.

EAR TRAINING Teaching the aural recognition of intervals, rhythms, etc., in an organized fashion.

ECHO The phenomenon of sound waves interacting with reflective surfaces, or the electronic simulation thereof. Also, repeating a passage at a lower dynamic level.

EIGHTH NOTE One eighth of a whole note. See Chapter 3.

EINHALT (Ger.) "Stop."

ELECTRONIC MUSIC Technically, music produced by electronic oscillators. By extension, any music requiring electrical energy.

EMBELLISHMENT (Fr.) Any ornamental musical device; e.g., **TRILL**, **GRACE NOTE**, etc.

EMBOUCHURE (Fr.) The facial muscles and their positions when playing a wind instrument.

ENCORE (Fr.) A repeat performance.

ENGLISH HORN See **COR ANGLAIS**.

ENHARMONIC TONES Those for whom there are alternate letter names; e.g., *F#* and *Gb*.

ENSEMBLE (Fr.) A group of performers. Also a direction for all to play together.

ENTR'ACTE (Fr.) A musical performance between the acts of a play or **OPERA**.

ENTRY The first statement by an individual or section within a musical piece.

EQUAL TEMPERAMENT A tuning system in use for European music since the 17th century, dividing the octave into 12 equal semitones.

ETHNOMUSICOLOGY The study of cultures through their music.

ETUDE (Fr.) A study or exercise written to improve a performer's technique.

EUPHONIUM	A brass instrument, pitched in *C* or *Bb*, designed to be a low **BARITONE** or high **TUBA**. Its frequency range is 64 Hz to 460 Hz; i.e., *C* to *bb'*.
EXPOSITION	The first statement of a musical theme.
EXPRESSION MARKS	Musical notation symbols indicating directions to the player; e.g., $\diagup$ (**CRESCENDO**). See Chapter 5.
EXTENDED HARMONY	A chord utilizing intervals beyond standard **TRIADS**. See Chapter 12.

F

....

F	The fourth step of the **C-MAJOR SCALE**. The frequency of *f'* above middle *C* is 352 Hz.
F-CLEF	The **BASS CLEF**, since it indicates *f* on the staff in the bass register. (*f* below middle *C* = 176 Hz.) See Chapter 4.
FAGOTT	(Ger.) The **BASSOON**.
FANDANGO	(Sp.) A traditional dance in three-four time.
FANFARE	A musical introduction, originally military or ceremonial, commonly scored for brass and/or percussion.
FANTASIA	(It.) A fanciful or fantasy composition without adherence to a particular format.
FERMATA	A musical notation symbol indicating "hold this note" until conductor indicates release. aka **BIRD'S EYE**: $\frown$
FIDDLE	Term for the **VIOLIN**, in the context of folk or country music.
FIFE	A "natural" flute, played transversely; i.e., blown horizontally across the opening. Originally used in European military field music. Pitched in various keys, made of wood, metal, or plastic; with a range between the **CONCERT FLUTE** and the **PICCOLO**.
FIGURED BASS	See **BASSO CONTINUO**.
FIN AL SEGNO	(It.) "Play from the beginning and finish at the sign."
FINE	(It.) "The end."

FINGERING	The position or sequence of finger motion to produce a particular note, phrase, or effect.
FIPPLE FLUTE	Any end-blown flute; e.g., a **RECORDER**.
FIRST INVERSION	A three-part chord (**TRIAD**) built with its third on the bottom, fifth in the middle, and root on top. See Chapter 12.
FLAG	Horizontal line drawn from the note stem to indicate rhythmic subdivision. See Chapter 3.
FLAGEOLET	(Latin/Fr.) Another name for the **RECORDER**. See **FIPPLE FLUTE**.
FLAMENCO	(Sp.) A Spanish dance, with origins in the Middle East (via the Moorish empire) and in Gypsy culture. Can be performed by solo, duet, or ensemble, the dancers adding percussive sounds via heel stomps, **CASTANETS**, and/or hand claps. Guitar and vocal accompaniment is traditional, with the vocalist also adding hand claps.
FLAT	An **ACCIDENTAL** used to indicate lowering of the following pitch by one half step. In the context of intonation, playing a pitch that is too low to be in tune.
FLOURISH	A **FANFARE**-like passage; an ornamental embellishment.
FLUGELHORN	(Ger.) A type of military **TRUMPET** with a more cylindrical bore than the **BUGLE** or **TRUMPET**, resulting in a darker, less strident tone than either. Its range is essentially that of the *Bb* **TRUMPET**, though it is rarely played in the extreme upper register which is quite difficult to control. Usable range: *e* (160 Hz) to *bb"* (920 Hz).
FLUTE	Technically, any transversely or end-blown wind instrument without a separate reed. The most common are the *C* **FLUTE** (Range: *c'* [middle *C*] (256 Hz) to *c""* (2,048 Hz), and the **ALTO FLUTE**, pitched in *G* (Range: *g* (198 Hz) to *g'''* (1,536 Hz).
FLUTTER TONGUE	A technique, used by wind players, of fluttering the tongue while playing, producing a rasping effect in the resulting sound.
FOLK MUSIC	Any music that is preserved by **ORAL TRADITION** and learned "by ear."
FORTE	(It.) "Loud." Abbr. *f*.

FORTISSIMO (It.) "Very loud." Abbr. *ff.*

FORZA, CON (It.) "With force," "forcefully," "with emphasis."

FORZANDO, FORZATO (It.) With strong accent. Also **SFORZANDO**, **SFORZATO**. Abbr. to **SFZ**.

FRENCH HORN The modern version of the **HUNTING HORN**, itself a refinement of the **RAM'S HORN** (**SHOFAR**). A brass instrument, usually pitched in the key of *F* with a conical bore and flaring bell, capable of chromatic playing, from *BB* (60 Hz) to *f'* (352 Hz).

FREQUENCY A determination of pitch based on the number of cycles-per-second (cps) or vibrations per second (vps) of a string, reed, membrane, column of air, or oscillator—mechanical or electrical. Standard musical pitch reference is *a'* [above middle *C*] = 440 **HERTZ** (Hz=cps=vps).

FRET A strip, usually made of metal or wood, set in the neck of a string instrument as a tactile guide for the performer, allowing the playing of discrete pitches.

FROG The handle of the **VIOLIN, VIOLA, CELLO** or **BASS** bow, containing the nut used to adjust the bow's tension.

FUGUE (Latin/Ger.) A sequential form of musical composition that was at its height of popularity during the Baroque period in Europe (1600-1750). Constructed for voice and/or instruments according to strict rules governing **SUBJECT** (theme), **RESPONSE** (answer in a key a fourth or fifth above), and **COUNTER SUBJECT** (original theme in a different voice and octave). During the response, a **COUNTERPOINT** is begun by the first voice, which is repeated by the second voice during the counter subject segment. Variations exist to this basic format.

FULL CADENCE Harmonic resolution from the **DOMINANT** to the **TONIC**. aka **AUTHENTIC CADENCE**. See Chapter 12.

FUNDAMENTAL The **ROOT** note of a chord or the principal pitch of a harmonic series.

FUNK In music, an expression derived from New Orleans street slang indicating a style that was deliberately not polished, but rather loose, syncopated, bluesy, and uninhibited.

FURIOSO (It.) "Furiously."

G   The fifth step of the **C-MAJOR SCALE**. The frequency of *g'* (above middle *C*) is 384 Hz.

G-CLEF   Another name for the **TREBLE CLEF**, it indicates the position of *G* on the staff (the clef curls around the *G* line) in the treble register (*g'* above middle *C*, 384 Hz).

GADULKA   A Bulgarian **FIDDLE**.

GALLIARDE   (Fr.) Lit. "merry." A dance in three-four time, popular in the 16th century.

GALLOP   (Fr.) A 19th century quick dance in three-four time.

GAMBA   (It.) Lit., "leg." Contraction for **VIOLA DA GAMBA**, the predecessor of the **CELLO**. The instrument is played at the leg, as opposed to the shoulder.

GAMELAN   The Indonesian percussion orchestra and/or the instruments thereof. Primarily made up of **METALLOPHONES** (each player generally playing two), tuned to **DIATONIC** and **PENTATONIC** scales, respectively.

GAPPED SCALE   One which divides the octave by less than seven steps; e.g., **PENTATONIC SCALE**, **WHOLE TONE SCALE**, etc.

GAVOTTE   (Fr.) A formalized version of a peasant dance, popular in 17th and 18th century Europe; set in four-four time, it usually begins on beat three.

GEHALTEN   (Ger.) Lit. "sustained." Indicates notes held to their full value.

GENERAL PAUSE   Abbreviated **G.P.**, an indication that the entire ensemble should rest for the time indicated.

GERMAN FLUTE   Another term for the transverse-blown flute, distinguishing it from end blown-types like the **RECORDER**.

GIGUE   (Fr.) A 17th century dance in six-eight time. Also a Medieval French **FIDDLE**.

GIOCONDO   (It.) "Joyfully," "merrily."

GITANA   (It.) A Gypsy dance.

GLASS HARMONICA A refinement of the concept of producing sounds by rubbing drinking glasses or glass bowls with moistened fingers. The instrument produces notes via a foot treadle that turns glass disks attached to spindles. The resulting harmonics are quite complex and extraordinarily difficult to reproduce on recording formats.

GLEE The predecessor of the modern Pop song. From Old English, meaning "entertainment," a short, harmonized vocal piece.

GLEE CLUB Originally, a vocal group active in London between 1787-1857. By extension, any large community vocal group.

GLISSANDO (It.) Slide from one note to another, playing all available pitches in between.

GLOCKENSPIEL (Ger.) Lit., "bells-play." The **BELL-LYRE**, a horizontal or vertical keyboard percussion instrument played with one or two mallets.

GONDOLIERA (It.) The song style associated with Venetian boatmen. aka **BARCAROLE**.

GONG Bronze, disk-shaped percussion instrument originating in Asia. Suspended from a frame and played with a single mallet. Produces an initial transient followed by a complex overtone series and a prolonged decay related to the force applied and the mass of the resonant disk.

GRACE NOTE An embellishment, written in smaller script and placed in front of the note to be enhanced. A slash through the grace note indicates that its duration not be counted metrically.

GRAN CASA (It.) The bass drum.

GRANDIOSO (It.) Play in a grand or regal manner.

GRAVE (It.) Solemn.

GREGORIAN CHANT See **CHURCH MODES**.

GRIOT (Fr.) The traditional itinerant African musician/storyteller, skilled at improvising verses over musical accompaniment. See **JALI**.

GROSSE FLOTE (Ger.) The standard, literally "large" **FLUTE**, as distinguished from the **KLEINE** (little) **FLOTE** (i.e. **PICCOLO**).

GROSSO	(It.) "Great," "grand."
GROUND BASS	See **BASSO OSTINATO**.
GUARACHA	(Sp.) An Afro-Cuban dance with meter and/or tempo changes.
GUIRO	(Sp.) A Latin percussion instrument made from a dried gourd. Slashes on the surface are scraped with a stick or comb.
GUITAR	The four, six, or 12-string instrument strummed and/or plucked. The range of the standard six-string guitar is *E* (80 Hz) to *a"* (880 Hz).
GUITARRON	(Sp.) The acoustic bass guitar in Mexican music.
GUITARILLO	(Port.) A small, four-string guitar.
GYPSY SCALES	Scales used in eastern European Gypsy folk music. Featuring either a flat second and sixth steps, or a flat third, raised fourth, and flat sixth. See Chapter 10.

H

H	In the German system, capital *H* indicates *B* natural, the capital *B* indicating *B*-flat.
HABANERA	A dance in a moderately slow two-four meter, whose underlying rhythm is traceable to the Middle East. The dance itself was popularized in Spain in the 1800's after being "re-introduced" from the Caribbean colonies. e.g.:

HALF CADENCE	Harmonic move from the **TONIC** to the **SUB-DOMINANT** or **DOMINANT**. aka **IMPERFECT CADENCE**. See Chapter 12.
HALF NOTE (OR REST)	In value, one half of a four-four measure; that is, one half of the value of the whole note (or rest). See Chapter 3.
HALF STEP	A semitone, or half tone, in the Western system.
HAND BELLS	The instruments used in a multi-player ensemble consisting of tuned clapper bells; Performers play multiple bells. Range for a 25-bell set is *g* (198 Hz) to *g"* (768 Hz).

HARMONICS	Whole-number multiples of the fundamental pitch. Also, related notes produced by damping certain strings on string instruments (e.g., guitar, harp, bass), or by over-blowing on some wind instruments. See Chapter 8.
HARMONICA	A common reed-type mouth organ.
HARMONIC MINOR	An alteration of the **DIATONIC MAJOR SCALE** with flat third and sixth steps. See Chapter 10.
HARMONIUM	A reed organ with a foot-controlled bellows. Range: C (64 Hz) to c'''' (2,048 Hz).
HARMONY	The vertical relationships among groups of pitches (or frequencies). See Chapters 8, 12.
HARP	Generic name given to a number of plucked string instruments. Also, a slang term for **HARMONICA** (**MOUTH HARP**). Also, the metal frame of the acoustic piano to which the strings are fastened. The modern harp (Cb double action) has a range of CCb (30 Hz) to cb'''' (3840 Hz). Pedals allow sets of strings to be tightened sufficiently to fluctuate by two semitones (one full step).
HARPSICHORD	A keyboard instrument that produces its sound by means of a plucking mechanism. The 18th century instrument has a range of FF (44 Hz) to f''' (1,408 Hz).
HAUTBOIS	(Fr.) [pron. "oh-bwa"] The **OBOE**.
HAWAIIAN GUITAR	See **STEEL GUITAR**.
HEAD TONES	Those of the **FALSETTO** range.
HELICON	An early form of the circular **TUBA**, or **SOUSAPHONE**. Range: FF (44 Hz) to bb (230 Hz).
HEMIDEMISEMIQUAVER	A 64th note, in the British notation system. See Chapter 3.
HETEROPHONY	Several performers simultaneously playing different variations of the same theme. Common technique in Japanese, Chinese, and Indonesian musics, as well as free jazz.
HOCKET	(Fr.) A 13th and 14th century composition device whereby each instrument is responsible for only one pitch, each time it occurs.

HOLD	Common term for **FERMATA**. ⌒
HOMOPHONY	Several performers playing or singing in unison. Also, having a clear emphasis on the melody.
HOOK	A repeated chorus, usually in a pop song.
HORN	Slang generic term for any wind instrument. In symphonic music, refers specifically to the **FRENCH HORN**.
HORNPIPE	A traditional British folk dance. Also, an instrument of Celtic origin with a single reed and one or two finger pipes.
HURDY GURDY	An instrument of Medieval origin, operated by a crank that turned a wheel, causing drone strings to vibrate while a keyboard produced melodies on the highest of the six strings.
HYMN	Generic term for a religious or spiritual piece of music.

I

....

IDEE FIXE	(Fr.) [pron. "ee-day-feex"] A short theme or motif (motive) quoted occasionally within a larger work.
IDIOPHONES	Fixed and indefinite pitch percussion instruments which are plucked, struck, rubbed, scraped, stamped upon, or shaken; e.g., **JAWBONE, MUSIC BOX, MARACAS**.
IMPERFECT CADENCE	Harmonic movement from the **TONIC** to the **SUB-DOMINANT** or **DOMINANT**. aka **HALF CADENCE**. See Chapter 12.
IMPRESSIONISM	In music, a style of European composition popular at the turn of the past century. Corresponding to the same period in the visual arts and sharing an orientation towards the abstract, the term originated in the subtitle of Claude Monet's painting "Sunrise." Maurice Ravel and Claude Debussy are considered Impressionist composers, though the latter disliked the term. Impressionist harmonies used consecutive fifths and fourths, considered improper by accepted popular composition rules at the time.
IMPROMPTU	Originally an interlude in a theatrical play. A written or guided "improvisation."
INCIDENTAL MUSIC	Background sub-score or other music fills between scenes or acts in a dramatic work. (See **INTERLUDES**.)

INSTRUMENT	Anything used to produce a musical sound event.
INSTRUMENTATION	Instrument voicing and distribution in an ensemble composition.
INTERLUDE	A short **INCIDENTAL** piece.
INTERMEZZO	(It.) An **INTERLUDE**.
INTERRUPTED CADENCE	aka **DECEPTIVE CADENCE**. Harmonic movement from the **DOMINANT** to any chord but the **TONIC**. See Chapter 12.
INTERVAL	The distance, based on whole and half steps, between any two pitches. See Chapters 8, 12.
INTONATION	Adherence to pitch relationships. "In-tune-ness."
INVERSION	Turning upside down an interval, chord, melody, or other musical device.
IONIAN MODE	See Chapter 10.
IRISH HARP	aka **CLARSECH**. A relatively small folk harp, plucked with fingernails rather than plectrums.
ISORHYTHM	A compositional device derived from the Medieval practice of repeating the melody in a different voice with a rhythmic variation. A modern equivalent in jazz is to perform the theme in double-time, in any voice other than the original lead.

J

JALI	(Mandinka) A member of the professional musician-storyteller class in the Gambia region of Africa. The status is inherited and includes social functions beyond entertainment. Jalis are exempt from taboos and social restraints, giving them a broad freedom of expression denied even to the nobility. See **GRIOT**.
JAWBONE	Originally, the actual lower jawbone of a jackass, used in Afro-Cuban percussion. It is either struck or scraped, causing the teeth to rattle. In contemporary ensembles the sound is produced by **VIBRA-SLAP** or **GUIRO**.

JAZZ A broad term for blues-based music, wholly or partially improvised. Can encompass dixieland, swing, be-bop, cool, avant-guard, latin jazz, jazz-rock, acid-jazz, and other crossover types.

JEW'S HARP aka **JAW HARP**. Small **LYRE**-shaped frame with a metal tongue which is plucked while the frame is held with the teeth. Varying the jaw position, lips, and mouth cavity produces varied tones.

JIG A Celtic folk dance. See **GIGUE**.

JONGLEUR (Fr.) In 11th to 13th century Europe, a generic term for entertainers; e.g., jugglers, dancers, musicians.

JUBILOSO (It.) Jubilant, celebratory.

K

KALIMBA (Bantu) The African thumb piano, aka **M'BIRA**, **SANSA**, **ZANZA**. A small gourd or wooden sound box or slab, over which are attached several metal or wooden tongues of various lengths. Some kalimbas have a bridge, which enables tuning by adjusting the tongue lengths. The resonator is held in both hands, and the tongues depressed then released by the thumbs, resulting in a twanging sound similar in texture to a **JAW HARP**, with rich upper harmonics.

KANON (Ger.) Canon.

KAPELMEISTER (Ger.) Chapel Master, Choir Director.

KAZOO A toy instrument. Essentially an open cylinder with a thin membrane placed 90 degrees to the air stream, which vibrates when the performer hums into the tube. Pitch is controlled by the player's vocal folds, the membrane imparting a buzzing texture to the sound.

KETTLE DRUMS The **TIMPANI**, large tunable drums with hemispherical metal shells. Each drum has a range of about a fifth, its parameters dictated by the diameter of the head. The range of a 30-inch timpanum is D (72 Hz) to A (110 Hz), 28-inch is F (88 Hz) to c (128 Hz), 25-inch is B (120 Hz) to f (174 Hz), 23-inch is d (144 Hz) to a (220 Hz). Drums are tuned by a crank mechanism, tuning screws around the head circumference or, usually, by a pedal.

KEY Any series of pitch relationships that suggest a tonal center or **TONIC** (**KEYNOTE**). Also, the mechanical levers on keyboard or wind instruments, or the individual alphabet and symbol finger pads used to command a computer in a musical situation (e.g. MIDI).

KEYBOARD Any instrument with a piano or organ-type key mechanism. Also, the mechanism itself.

KEYNOTE The **TONIC** or tonal center pitch of any key.

KEY SIGNATURE The placement and number of sharps or flats after the clef on the staff indicating the tonal center of the music to follow. See Chapter 11.

KICK Slang term for the bass drum in a drum set, which is played by a foot pedal.

KIT Slang term for a drum set. Also, an obsolete "pocket violin" with three strings.

KLAVIER (Ger.) **PIANOFORTE, HARPSICHORD**.

KONZERTMEISTER (Ger.) Concertmaster, usually the principal violinist.

KOTO A Japanese **ZITHER** with 13 strings and moveable bridges. Tuning is usually **PENTATONIC**. Plectrums are attached to the fingers of the player who sits with the instrument placed horizontally. Range is roughly equivalent to the standard guitar: E (80 Hz) to a" (880 Hz).

KYRIE (Greek) Lord. The first movement in the formal musical mass.

L ....

LARGAMENTE (It.) Broadly.

LARGHETTO (It.) A tempo designation of approx. 72 to 98 beats per minute.

LARGO (It.) A tempo designation of between 44 to 70 beats per minute.

LEADING TONE The seventh note of any scale, major or minor. aka **SUBTONIC**.

LEGATO (It.) Smooth.

LEGER LINES	Short lines placed above or below a staff, to designate pitches outside the staff range. Alternate spelling: **LEDGER**.
LEITMOTIF, LEITMOTIV	(Ger.) A short theme, melody, or rhythm that recurs throughout a larger work and is identified with a particular character, place, emotion, etc.
LENTO	(It.) Slow. A tempo designation between 60 to 70 beats per minute.
LIBRETTO	(It.) The book or text of an **OPERA** or similar work.
LIED	(Ger.) Song. A ballad with lyrics.
LIGATURE	The metal apparatus that holds the reed of a woodwind instrument in place.
LOCO	(Latin) In place. Play as written. Cancels an **OTTAVA** (**OCTAVA**).
LUTE	The forerunner of the modern guitar, mandolin, etc. The body is pear-shaped and originally had five strings. The modern lute has 11 strings, 10 of which are double. Tuning range is G (96 Hz) to g' (384 Hz), this highest note being a single string.
LYDIAN MODE	See Chapter 10.
LYRE	An ancient harp-like instrument from the Middle East and Mediterranean.
LYRIC	The words, the verbal component of a song.

M

MADRIGAL	A song form originating in 14th century Europe, originally for two voices; later types used up to six parts.
MAESTOSO	(It.) Majestic.
MAESTRO	(It.) Master. A title of respect. A master musician, composer, or conductor.
MALAGUEÑA	(Sp.) A song type associated with the city of Malaga, in Spain. Usually in three-four time.

MANDOLIN (It.) A strummed instrument derived from the **LUTE**, featuring eight strings, tuned in doubles. Range is *g* (198 Hz) to *a'''* (1,760 Hz).

MARACAS (Sp.) An Afro-Cuban percussion instrument made from gourds filled with pebbles. Handles are attached and the instruments are played in pairs.

MARCATO (It.) A direction to play each note with a marked accent.

MARIACHI (Sp.) A Mexican folk singer/guitarist or group of similar singers, sometimes augmented by violins, trumpets, **GUITARRON**, and harp.

MARIMBA An African **XYLOPHONE** with tuned wooden bars or keys. The modern instrument uses rosewood keys and metal resonators. It has a four-octave range, from *c* (128 Hz) to *c"* (512 Hz). The bass marimba's range is *CC* (64 Hz) to *c'* (256 Hz).

MASQUE (Fr.) A forerunner of the modern **OPERA**, originating in 16th century Europe. A musical masquerade performed for the nobility, usually featuring singing, dancing, and drama.

MEASURE In a composition, the music contained between bar lines. Technically, the terms "bar" and "measure" are not identical, but it is common practice to use the terms interchangeably.

MEDIANT The third step, or degree, of the **DIATONIC SCALE**. See Chapter 10.

MEDIEVAL A historical period, the Middle Ages in Europe, extending from about 500-1500 a.d.

MEDLEY A group of similar songs performed sequentially.

MEISTERSINGERS Members of German musical guilds formed to continue the tradition of the earlier **MINNESINGERS (TROUBADOURS)**, a European version of the African **GRIOTS**, organized by the aristocracy to produce heroic ballads about the aristocrats' exploits and/or virtues. Minnesingers (1150-1450 a.d.) sang in unison (or solo), without harmony. Meistersingers (1450-1600) sought to preserve these traditions.

MELISMA (Greek) The technique of singing a number of notes on one vowel syllable.

MELLOPHONE	A hybrid brass instrument roughly equivalent to the **FRENCH HORN**. Its timbre is brighter, due to its trumpet-like cup (rather than conical) mouthpiece. It employs piston valves rather than rotaries. Practical range: *B* (120 Hz) to *f"* (704 Hz).
MELODEON	A kind of button **ACCORDION** or **CONCERTINA**.
MELODICA	Instrument combining the actions of a keyboard and a woodwind to produce a sound similar to the **HARMONICA**.
MELODIC MINOR SCALE	An alteration of the **DIATONIC MAJOR SCALE** featuring a flat third and natural seventh (leading tone) when ascending, and a flat seventh, sixth, and third when descending. See Chapter 10.
MELODY	(Greek) Any sequence or succession of pitches that can be recognized as a unit. Also, the lead (usually highest) line in any harmonized composition.
MENSURAL NOTATION	A Medieval system of note values originating in Germany about 1250 a.d., in use in European music until around 1600. See Chapters 2, 3.
METER, METRE	A general pattern or outline of stressed and unstressed beats, regularly appearing throughout a musical work. aka **TIME SIGNATURE**.
METRONOME	A device that produces aural or visual beat references for establishing tempo. The mechanical version was patented in 1816 by Johann Maezel in Germany. Beethoven and Czerny were prominent advocates, using metronome markings to indicate exact tempos for their works. (e.g. ♩=120 = 120 quarter note beats per minute) Electronic metronomes are common today.
MEZZO FORTE	(It.) Medium or half loud. Abbr. *mf.*
MEZZO PIANO	(It.) Medium or half soft. Abbr. *mp.*
MEZZO SOPRANO	(It.) Medium soprano. A female voice range between alto and soprano. Range from middle *C* [*c'*] (256 Hz) to *g"* (768 Hz).
MIDDLE C	aka *C* **PRIME** or the *c'* at the center of the piano keyboard. Frequency: 256 Hz (cycles per second).
MILITARY BAND	Originally, a British regimental band with brass, percussion, and woodwinds. An older term for concert or symphonic band.

MINIATURE SCORE	Complete notation for a given piece of music, inclusive of all parts, vocal and instrumental, reduced in size for convenience of study.
MINIM	In British musical terminology, a half note. See Chapter 3.
MINNESINGERS	German **TROUBADOURS** of the Medieval period. Minnesingers composed and sang epic ballads and heroic folk songs, as a solo or in monophonic unison. The predecessors of the **MEISTERSINGERS** and originators of the tradition of group singing that endures today in beer-hall and college fight songs.
MINOR	A scale, chord, or interval that varies from its **MAJOR** counterpart by being reduced by one or more half steps (semitones). See Chapters 8, 10, 12.
MINSTREL	The English term for **TROUBADOUR**. A folk singer/entertainer of the Medieval period. Also, name adopted by late 19th and early 20th century American vaudeville entertainers who performed musical skits.
MINUET	A dance in three-four time, popular in 17th and 18th century Europe, having originated in the French court in 1650. Quite slow and formal by modern standards.
MISTERIOSO	(It.) Indicates the passage is to be played "mysteriously." Often encountered in film and TV scores.
MIXOLYDIAN MODE	See Chapter 10.
MIXED METER	Music containing time signatures that change frequently, in a sequential pattern.
MODE	(Latin) Literally, "manner," or "type." Referring to the **CHURCH MODES** themselves (see Chapter 10), or other scales derived or reminiscent of same.
MODERATO	(It.) "Moderate," "moderately."
MODULATION	Moving from one key center to another within a piece of music.
MOLL	(Ger) "Minor."

MONOCHORD (Greek) Lit., "one string." An ancient instrument in use by 500 b.c., used to measure string vibration and the mathematical frequency relationships between various intervals. Consisting of a single string, sound box, and movable bridge.

MONOTONE (Greek) Singing or speaking several words or syllables in a single pitch, without melodic inflection.

MORDENT An ornamentation or embellishment to a single note, comprising a pattern of adjacent pitches. A musical shorthand symbol directing such embellishment. See Chapter 5.

MOTET A type of vocal music originating in Medieval Europe as an outgrowth of **PLAINSONG** (**CHANT**). Significant in that, over time, **COUNTERPOINT** and **POLYPHONY** (harmony) were introduced, forming the basic structure of modern Western music.

MOTIF (Fr.) "Theme." Short rhythmic and/or melodic fragment appearing occasionally within a musical work. aka **MOTIVE**, **LEITMOTIF**.

MOUTH ORGAN **HARMONICA**.

MOVEMENT A distinct section of a larger musical work, like a **CONCERTO** or **SYMPHONY**. Each movement generally has its own rhythmic, harmonic, and melodic identity.

MULTIPLE STOP aka multi-stop, double stop, triple stop. String playing technique wherein two or more strings are sounded simultaneously, producing an interval or chord. Also, in organ playing, the use of more than one manually operated effect switch. "Pulling out all the stops" would produce the most complex and loudest sound possible on the instrument.

MUSETTE (Fr.) A French **BAGPIPE** popular from the 17th century. A type of de-tuning on some accordions and synthesizers, wherein three pitches are sounded at once—the true pitch, one slightly **SHARP**, and one slightly **FLAT**.

MUSIC BOX A mechanical form of thumb piano wherein a spring-operated cylinder with protruding pins rotates against a tuned metal comb, plucking melody, harmony, and rhythm. The idea of mechanical sound reproduction led ultimately to the phonograph.

MUSICOLOGY The study of the philosophy of music, or musical anthropology; its history, origins, effect on society, society's effect on music, aesthetics, and cultural importance.

MUSIQUE CONCRÈTE (Fr.) A recording of natural sounds and/or ambiences, sequenced and processed to give a random or arbitrary effect.

MUTE Any device used to reduce the dynamic level and/or alter the timbre of an instrument. Significant in recording, since overtones and harmonics will be radically affected (EQ), and the point of sound emanation from the instrument (source) may be relocated.

N

NACHTMUSIK (Ger.) "Night Music," **NOCTURNE**.

NATURAL A musical symbol ♮ that cancels a preceding **SHARP** or **FLAT**. Also, a distinct musical pitch (frequency) referred to by its letter name, and which appears without a sharp (♯) or flat (♭) sign preceding it.

NATURAL HORN A wind instrument derived from an animal horn (e.g., **SHOFAR**), or bone structure (**CONCH SHELL**), or any human-made horn without valves or keys (e.g., **HUNTING HORN**). Such instruments are capable of producing their fundamental resonance frequency and natural overtone series. A natural horn played in its lower register produces only wide intervals (e.g., octaves, fifths, thirds).

NECK The fingerboard of a string instrument.

NEIGHBORING TONE One which is one scale step away from a given pitch.

NEO-CLASSICISM In art or music, creating a modern composition in a Classical style; using forms and techniques of the Classical period to produce new works. Also, any revival of Classical methods, subject matter, etc.

NEUME (Latin) A form of musical notation used in Medieval European **CHANTS** and **PLAINSONG**. Originally, neumes indicated approximate pitch, not duration. Eventually evolved into the standard notation in current use. See Chapters 3, 4.

NOCTURNE (Fr.) Night Music, a **SERENADE**.

NODES The points on a vibrating string that, when touched, produce harmonics (whole number multiples) related to the frequency of the fundamental. Nodes also exist in air columns in wind instruments and are accessed by vibrating the lips or reed at or near the node frequencies. Also, the natural harmonics (resonant frequencies which are whole number multiples of the fundamental) inherent in any length of string or tube or enclosed space.

NONHARMONIC TONE Any pitch outside the given key, whether it appears melodically (e.g., **GRACE NOTE**), or harmonically (e.g., a chord with a flat fifth).

NON TROPPO (It.) "Not too much."

NOTATION A system of depicting musical information visually, with written symbols. See Chapters 3, 4.

NUT A notched ridge at the top of a string instrument that guides the string between the tuning pegs and the **NECK**. Also, the device that adjusts the tension of the bow.

O

O When printed in lower-case on a score, indicates playing a note "open." Some instruments can achieve the same pitch with a variety of fingerings, but the textures and frequencies are subtly different. Also, the physical demands on the performer may be a factor in choosing one fingering over another.

OBBLIGATO (It.) Literally, "obligatory." A **CONTRAPUNTAL** theme, complementary to the main melody and, theoretically, necessary to the structure of the piece as a whole. Usually written above the main melody (e.g., the **FALSETTO** background to the lead voice in **A CAPELLA** singing).

OBOE The end-blown double reed woodwind instrument in the contemporary orchestra or symphonic band. Its range is from *bb* (230 Hz) to *g'''* (1536 Hz).

OCARINA (It.) A ceramic "sweet potato" shaped whistle with finger holes. A folk instrument made in various keys and found in many cultures under numerous names. Timbre approximates the **RECORDER**.

OCTAVE (Latin) "Eight." In music, an interval at a distance of eight **DIATONIC** pitches; the interval between a given pitch and one at twice its frequency:

1	2	3	^	4	5	6	7	^	8
DO	RE	MI	^	FA	SO	LA	TI	^	DO
C	*D*	*E*	^	*F*	*G*	*A*	*B*	^	*c*

In the major scale, half steps (semitones) separate steps 3 and 4, and 7 and 8. This structure evolved from commonly accepted octave divisions in early Western European music systems. Other cultures divide the "octave" into fewer, more, or different intervals. See Chapters 4, 8, 10, 11, 12.

OCTAVE MARKS **8va** (**OTTAVA**) over a note or phrase is an indication to play it one octave higher than written (acoustically expressed as doubling of all frequencies). **8vb** (**OTTAVA BASSA**) is an instruction to play the passage one octave lower than written. **LOCO** (place) cancels 8va/8vb, and directs a return to the written octave.

OCTET A group of eight players or vocalists. Also, a composition arranged for such a group, with eight distinct parts.

OPEN HARMONY Voicing a chord such that there are wide gaps between the component pitches.

OPEN STRING, TONE See, "**0**," above.

OPERA A drama in musical form. Origin of European opera dates from Renaissance Italy. The **GRAND OPERA** has music throughout, without spoken **RECITATIVE**. **OPERA COMIQUE** includes spoken passages but is not necessarily comedic. **OPERA BOUFFE** (**BUFFA**) is farcical and includes recitative. **OPERA LYRIQUE** (**OPERETTA**) intersperses songs with dialogue and is the direct predecessor of the "Broadway" musical.

OPUS (Latin) A work, a piece. Abbr. **Op**.

ORCHESTRA (Greek) Literally, "place for dancing." Today the term has multiple meanings: The **SYMPHONY ORCHESTRA** with strings, woodwinds, brass and percussion; any large musical group; the ground level seating in the concert hall, nearest the musicians.

ORCHESTRAL SCORE A copy of the complete musical work, showing all individual parts.

ORCHESTRATION	The act of organizing a musical work by assigning its elements to particular instruments or voices. If the original music is altered substantially in form, melody, harmony, rhythm, etc., it becomes an **ARRANGEMENT** of the original material.
ORGAN	Generic name for a number of keyboard instruments: The **PIPE ORGAN** is powered by air pressure pushed through tubes of various sizes; the **REED ORGAN** (including **HARMONICA, CONCERTINA, HARMONIUM,** and **ACCORDION**) by passing air through tuned reeds; the **ELECTRIC ORGAN** produces oscillations which are then modified and amplified. Some pipe organs are capable of a nine-octave range from *CCC* (16 Hz) to *c''''''* (8,192 Hz).
ORGANUM	(Latin) Two-part singing developed in European liturgical music around the 9th century. The origin of **POLYPHONY**.
ORNAMENT	An embellishment to a note or phrase. See **SYMBOLS**, Chapter 5.
OVERBLOWING	A technique of increasing the air pressure in some wind instruments that results in the sounding of harmonics rather than the fundamental pitch. These alternate fingerings can produce the approximate desired frequencies, but will vary in timbre and dynamic level from the same pitches played in the standard position.
OVERTONES	aka **HARMONICS, PARTIALS**. A particular set of frequencies, including but not limited to harmonics, that are related to the fundamental pitch being played. The relationship between these frequencies to the fundamental determines the timbre, or tone color, of the resultant sound. Alteration in EQ of frequencies beyond the actual range of the instruments results in a different "tone."
OVERTURE	A musical introduction to a longer work, previewing thematic material in capsule form. Also, a work written in a single movement form. See **SONATA FORM**.

P

PAN PIPES	aka **REED PIPES**. An end-blown wind instrument, common to many cultures, consisting of hollow reeds of graduated lengths, lashed side by side. Tuning and range vary.
PARLANDO	(It.) "Speak." Perform the music with speech-like inflection.

PARODY	The comic or satiric imitation of another work.
PARTIAL	See **OVERTONES**.
PASSACAGLIA	(It.) A European dance of the Baroque period (1600-1750), in three-four time with a **BASSO OSTINATO**.
PASSAGE	Generic term for a short segment of music.
PASTORALE	(It.) A musicical composition written to suggest a rural scene.
PAUSA	(It.) "Pause," "rest."
PAVANE	(Fr.) A 16th century Italian dance modified by the French to include slow and fast sections.
PEDAL	Abbr. **PED**. Foot levers of the piano, harp, timpani. Also, the foot-operated damper of the vibraphone or chime.
PEDAL TONE	In wind instruments, the fundamental or lowest possible pitch (acoustically, produced by the entire length of the pipe).
PEGS	Adjustable pins on string instruments that facilitate tuning.
PENNY WHISTLE	aka **TIN WHISTLE**. A Celtic end-blown instrument with fingerholes. Made in various keys.
PENTATONIC SCALE	A a scale that divides the **OCTAVE** into five steps. Common to many cultures. Any five-note scale.
PERCUSSION	Instruments whose sound is produced by shaking, striking, or scratching. Also, the section of the orchestra comprising these instruments.
PERFECT CADENCE	aka **AUTHENTIC, FULL, COMPLETE CADENCE**. Harmonic movement from the **DOMINANT** (V) to the **TONIC** (I). See Chapter 12.
PERFECT PITCH	aka **ABSOLUTE PITCH**. The ability to distinguish the pitch of a note by ear.
PETITE FLUTE	**PICCOLO**.
PHRASE	A musical idea.
PHRASING	The manner in which phrases of music are expressed by the performer.

PHRYGIAN MODE One of the Medieval **CHURCH MODES**. See Chapter 10.

PIANO Shortened form of the keyboard instrument whose full name is **PIANOFORTE**. The standard modern piano has a range from *AAA* (22.5 HZ) to *c'''''* (4,096 Hz). Also, "soft" in Italian. Abbr. **p.**

PICCOLO (It.) The highest-pitched flute. Range: *d"* (576 Hz) to *c'''''* (4,096 Hz).

PICK A plectrum; small chip of hard material used to pluck strings.

PICK-UP Note or group of notes leading to an emphasized note or beat. (also, **ANACRUSIS**). Also, the small electronic device (microphone) used to transform guitar or bass string vibrations into analogous electrical energy.

PITCH The musical term for frequency. May be expressed in hertz, cycles-per-second, vibrations-per-second, or by note letter name.

PITCH PIPE A wind-blown device capable of producing reference pitches for tuning.

PIZZACATO (It.) Plucking, as opposed to bowing or strumming a string instrument. Abbr. **pizz.**

PLAGAL CADENCE Harmonic movement from the **SUBDOMINANT** (IV) to the **TONIC** (I). See Chapter 12.

PLAINSONG aka **PLAINCHANT. MONOPHONIC** (one-part) vocal music based upon **CHURCH MODES**.

POCO (It.) "Little," "a little."

POLKA A folk dance in two-four, originating in Eastern Europe.

POLONAISE (Fr.) A dance from Poland featuring a three-four **OSTINATO** rhythm. See Chapter 3.

POLYMETER Music featuring at least two simultaneous time signatures (meters).

POLYPHONY A form of harmony achieved by the use of at least two simultaneous melodies.

POLYTONAL MUSIC A modern composition technique based on at least three simultaneous keys (tonal centers).

PONTICELLO	(It.) The bridge of a bowed string instrument.
PORTAMENTO	(It.) The technique of sliding seamlessly between two discrete pitches over a wide interval.
POSTLUDE	Ending music, exit music, "outro."
POUSSEZ	(Fr.) Up bow.
PRELUDE	Opening music, beginning music, intro.
PREMIERE	(Fr.) The first performance, a debut.
PRESTO	(It.) "Fast," "quick." Indicates a tempo between 186 and 208 beats per minute, approximately.
PROGRAM MUSIC	Instrumental compositions which, theoretically, suggest a setting, mood, or sequence of events. Film and video sub-score. Opposite of **ABSOLUTE MUSIC**.
PROGRESSION	Harmonic: moving from one chord to the next; a sequence of chord changes. Melodic: the sequential note movement of a melody.
PULSE	Non-specific term referring to tempo, rhythm, or accented beat.
PYTHAGOREAN TUNING	A tuning system devised by Greek astronomer and mathematician Pythagoras about 600 b.c.; a division of the **OCTAVE** based on calculations of the rates of vibrating strings. In use in Europe until about 1500 a.d.

Q

QUADRUPLE METER	Any time signature with four beats to a measure.
QUADRUPLET	A mathematically artificial grouping of four equal notes played in the time frame given for three of the same value. See Chapter 3.
QUARTER NOTE	Musical notation representing one quarter of a whole note's value.
QUARTER REST	The rest equivalent to the **QUARTER NOTE**, equal in value.

QUARTER TONE	aka **QUARTER STEP**. An interval of half a semitone. Common to many non-Western tuning systems. See Chapters 4, 10, 12.
QUARTET	An ensemble of four voices or players. Also any music written for four distinct parts.
QUASI	(It.) "Almost."
QUAVER	An eighth note, in the British music notation system. See Chapter 3.
QUIJADA	(Sp.) The percussion instrument known in English as the **JAW BONE**.
QUINTET	An ensemble of five voices or players. Also, any music written for five distinct parts.
QUINTUPLE METER	Any time signature with five beats to the measure.
QUINTUPLET	A mathematically artificial grouping of five equal notes played in the time frame given for four of the same value.

R
....

R	Abbreviation for "right" or "right hand."
RAGA	A type of Indian music, designed for ritual, featuring vocal or instrumental melody over a **DRONE**. Principal instruments include **SITAR**, **TAMBURA**, and **TABLAS**.
RAGTIME	Name given to a syncopated style of American popular music originating in New Orleans in the 1890's. The concept of time was somewhat fluid, hence *ragged*, by traditional standards.
RALLENTANDO	(It.) Slow gradually, without decreasing intensity. Abbr. **Rall.**
RANGE	Refers to the practical frequency compass of a voice or instrument.
RECAPITULATION	The repeating of a theme (usually in the context of **SONATA FORM**).
RECITAL	A solo performance. Also, a performance featuring a primary soloist with accompanist(s).

RECITATIVE Song-like speech. Common element of **OPERA**.

RECORDER A refinement of the end-blown flute, with a sculptured ligature and standardized tuning and technique. aka **FIPPLE FLUTE, FLAGOLET, BLOCK FLUTE, BEAK FLUTE, ENGLISH FLUTE**. Modern recorders are of six types:
- **SOPRANINO**—f'' (704 Hz) to f'''' (2,816 Hz)
- **SOPRANO**—c'' (512 Hz) to c'''' (2,048 Hz)
- **ALTO**—f' (352 Hz) to f''' (1,408 Hz)
- **TENOR**—c' (256 Hz) to c''' (1,024 Hz).
- **BASS**—f (176 Hz) to f'' (704) Hz.
- **CONTRABASS**—c (128 Hz) to c'' (512 Hz)

REDUCTION A complete score reduced to small type, used for study/review.

REED A membrane, set in motion by air stream (vibrated), producing a sound. Reed instruments are classified as:
- **FREE REED**: harmonica, accordion.
- **SINGLE REED**: clarinet, saxophone.
- **DOUBLE REED**: oboe, bassoon, English horn.

REEL Originally, a Celtic folk dance for groups of couples. Popular in Northern Europe. Brought to the U.S. by colonization.

REFRAIN The **CHORUS**; the repeated part of a song.

REGISTER aka **RANGE**. A section (i.e. upper, lower) of the range of a voice or instrument. In organ playing, the effects on voices associated with a given stop.

RELATIVE PITCH The ability to accurately identify intervals by ear, based on their relationships to given pitches.

RENAISSANCE (Fr.) "Rebirth." Historical period in Europe between 1450-1600 a.d. Also, any artistic revitalization.

REPEAT SIGNS In music notation, signs indicating a repeat of the section between them. See Chapter 5.

REPRISE (Fr.) A repeat of an important theme. Also, an **ENCORE**.

RESOLUTION A relative term meaning a conclusion of some type, temporary or final.

RESONATOR	Technically, anything that responds to vibration. Also, any acoustical reinforcement that increases resonance; e.g., hollow tubes below vibraphone keys.
RESPONSE	The answer to a call or to the statement of the subject, vocally or instrumentally.
REST	A notation symbol indicating silence for a specified time. See Chapter 3.
RETROGRADE	Indicating the performing of a given melody, rhythm, or harmony backwards.
RHAPSODY	Nonspecific term for a highly expressive, relatively short composition.
RHYTHM	A pattern of stressed and unstressed beats varying in duration or placement in time. See Chapter 3.
RHYTHM&BLUES	aka **R&B**. A catch-all marketing term, invented by radio programmers and recording companies, used to describe several types of black American music.
RICOCHET	(Fr.) Indication to a string player to "bounce" the bow.
RIFF	Generic jazz/rock term for a melodic or rhythmic theme, especially one that is repeated.
RITARDANDO	(It.) Direction to slow the tempo. Abbr. *rit.*
ROCK AND ROLL	aka **ROCK 'N ROLL, ROCK**. Generic commercial term for popular American music evolving from a mix of blues and other forms during the 1950's. Amplified electric guitars and vocal sound reinforcement featured.
ROCOCO	(Fr.) An ornamented style of music of the late **BAROQUE** (18th century) period.
ROMANTICISM	European compositional style popular in the 19th century as an evolution of **CLASSICISM**. Characterized by use of chromatic harmonies and melodies and exaggerated (theoretically emotional) dynamics.
RONDO	(It.) Formula for composition calling for four short sections, thematically related, with connecting interludes.

ROOT The **TONIC**, or letter name, by which a chord is known. See Chapter 12.

ROUND A type of composition, usually vocal, wherein overlapping voices enter sequentially, exactly repeating the melody as stated by the first voice.

RUBATO (It.) "Robbed." A direction to play interpretively, with freedom of rhythm.

RUMBA (Sp.) (also **RHUMBA**) A Cuban dance popularized in the U.S. in the 1930's and 40's. Forerunner of the Mambo craze of the 50's.

RUN Slang term for a technically complex musical passage.

S

SACKBUT (Ger.) The medieval **TROMBONE**.

SALTANDO (It.) Also **SALTATO**. An indication for string players to play with short, bouncy strokes, using the upper part of the bow.

SAMBA (Port.) A popular Afro-Brazilian dance in two-four time.

SAMISEN (Japanese) Name for a group of three string **LUTE**-type instruments. Played with a plectrum. aka **SHAMISEN**.

SANSA Alternate name for the **KALIMBA**, African thumb-piano. aka **MBIRA**, **ZANZA**.

SANTUR The Turkish **HAMMER DULCIMER**, Greek **SANTOURI**, Arabian **SANTIR**.

SAROD A **LUTE**-shaped **FIDDLE** from India and Persia. Range: c' (256 Hz) to c''' (1024 Hz), approximately.

S.A.T.B. Standard abbreviation for vocal parts **SOPRANO, ALTO, TENOR,** and **BASS**.

SAXHORNS Keyed bugles developed by Adolphe Sax in the 1840's. Some still in use. See **BUGLE**.

SAXOPHONE Name given to the group of single-reed brasswinds invented by Adolphe Sax. The four most common are:
- *Bb* **SOPRANO**: ab (210 Hz) to eb''' (1216 Hz)
- *Eb* **ALTO**: db (136 Hz) to ab'' (824 Hz)

- **Bb TENOR**: *ab* (105 Hz) to *Eb"* (608 Hz)
- **Eb BARITONE**: *Db* (68 HZ) to *ab'* (412 Hz).

SCALE   Generic name for the succession of notes subdividing an octave. See Chapter 10.

SCHERZO   (It.) A quick, energetic piece of music. Originally, the third movement of a **SONATA** or **SYMPHONY**. Usually in triple meter.

SCORE   Complete musical notation showing all parts of an ensemble, either combined or on separate staves.

SECULAR MUSIC   Technically, any music not intended for religious services.

SELECTIVE HEARING   The ability or propensity of the human auditory system to filter out unwanted or unnecessary audio information.

SEMIBREVE   In British music notation system, a whole note. See Chapter 3.

SEMIQUAVER   In the British music notation system, a 16th note. See Chapter 3.

SEMITONE   In the common Western chromatic tuning, an interval of a half step/minor second. See Chapters 4, 10, 12.

SEMPLICE   (It.) Play simply, without embellishment.

SEMPRE   (It.) "Continually," "always;" e.g., **SEMPRE PIANO**: "always soft."

SENZA   (It.) "Without."

SEPTET   A group of seven performers. Also music written for seven distinct parts.

SEPTUPLET   An artificial (mathematically) grouping of seven notes of equal value. See Chapter 3.

SEQUENCE   The repetition of a given melodic or rhythmic pattern, beginning on a different pitch each time.

SERENADE   (Fr.) Originally, an evening love song. Any piece reminiscent of such music.

SERIES   A method of composing music using the 12-tone (chromatic) scale and a numerical sequencing formula. aka **TONE ROW, TWELVE-TONE ROW**.

SEXTET A group of six performers. Also, music written with six distinct parts.

SEXTUPLET A(mathematically) artificial grouping of six notes of equal value. See Chapter 3.

SFORZANDO (It.) aka **SFORZATO**. An indication to strongly accent the beginning of a note or phrase. Abbr. *sfz*.

SFORZANDO PIANO (It.) Abbr. *sfzp*. An indication to quickly soften the remainder of a note or phrase immediately following the initial accent.

SHAKE aka **LIP TRILL**. A brass playing technique of slurring rapidly and continuously between two pitches, without finger movement.

SHANTY aka **CHANTEY**. A seaman's work song. Common to numerous cultures.

SHARP In notation, an **ACCIDENTAL** indicating raising the given pitch by a half-step; in intonation, playing a pitch that is too high to be in tune.

SHAWM An ancient double-reed instrument from the Middle East. The inspiration for the **OBOE** and **BASSOON**.

SHENG (Chinese) An ancient wind instrument consisting of a gourd and reed pipes. A true **MOUTH ORGAN**, produces tones by inhalation and exhalation. Various keys and ranges. Japanese **SHO**.

SHOFAR The **RAM'S HORN** of the ancient Hebrews. Common to most hunting cultures. Together with the conch shell, the antecedent of all horns.

SIDE DRUM aka **SNARE DRUM**. Any of a variety of drums, originally for military use, with vibrating strings or snares across one or both heads, emphasizing the high frequency partials of the resonating head and shell.

SIGHT READING (SINGING) The technique of performing the music by reading the printed page without prior hearing.

SIMILE (Latin) Continue to carry out previous direction. In a similar fashion.

SINFONIA (It.) A **SYMPHONY**, usually written for a small orchestra.

SINFONIETTA   (It.) A short symphony.

SITAR   The traditional string instrument of India. In use by the 14th century. Sound is produced via drone and melody strings stretched above a gourd-like hollow wood body with sound holes. Usually tuned outside the twelve-tone Western system.

SLIDE   The moveable portion of the **TROMBONE**'s tubing. Also, any number of tuning joints on wind instruments. Also, the technique of moving the finger (or a comb, bottle-neck, etc.) smoothly along the neck of a string instrument, or the implement used for this technique.

SLIDE TRUMPET   Actually, a **SOPRANO TROMBONE**. A trumpet played with a slide mechanism, as opposed to valves. Range corresponds to the standard *Bb* trumpet, approximately *e* (160 Hz) to *c'''* (1,024 Hz).

SLIDE WHISTLE   A **RECORDER**-like flute without finger holes. Pitch is altered by a movable slide inside the tube. Range varies with length.

SLUR   A musical notation symbol directing the player to connect all notes below the curved line smoothly and seamlessly, i.e. without distinct articulation.

SNARE DRUM   See **SIDE DRUM**.

SOCK CYMBAL   Alternate term for **HI-HAT**, the pedal-operated cymbal in a drum kit.

SOLFEGE (Fr.), **SOLFEGGIO** (It.)   The technique of teaching music reading and ear training through the vocalization of syllables: *DO, RE, MI,* etc.

SONATA FORM   A basic structure common in music composition, consisting of three sections: **EXPOSITION** of melodic material, **DEVELOPMENT**, and **RECAPITULATION**.

SOPRANO   The highest female singing range. Range: *eb'* (300 Hz) to *bb''* (920 Hz).

SORDINO   (It.) Mute. Any of a number of devices that reduce the amplitude and alter the timbre of an instrument. Also, a direction to employ such a device (i.e. "**CON SORDINO**").

SOSTENUTO   (It.) Sustain notes for their full value, without shortening.

SOTTO VOCE   (It.) "Under the voice." Sing or play softly, like a whisper.

SOUND Any change in atmospheric pressure level perceptible to the ear. Also, any measurable atmospheric wave phenomenon.

SOUND BOARD Thin resonating layer of wood within the piano whose vibration reinforces the string tones. Also, any similar resonating chamber in an instrument.

SOUND HOLE aka *F-HOLE*. An opening in the resonating chamber of a string instrument or piano.

SOUSAPHONE A portable, bell-front, wrap-around-the-player **TUBA** developed for John Philip Sousa's band. Range *FF* (44 Hz) to *bb* (230 Hz).

SPINET A relatively small, upright piano with full keyboard. A rehearsal piano.

STACCATO (It.) An indication to play the notes of a passage short and separated. Opposite of **LEGATO**.

STAFF (STAVE) A grid consisting of five horizontal lines and four spaces, for the purpose of annotating musical pitch.

STEEL BAND A type of percussion ensemble originating in Trinidad. Discarded oil containers are crafted into tunable steel drums of various sizes and ranges, each capable of producing several discrete tones.

STEEL GUITAR aka **HAWAIIAN GUITAR, PEDAL STEEL**. An electric guitar with single or double neck, played across the lap with plectra and steel bar or "bottle" slide. Range corresponds to standard electric guitar. Tuned in chords, rather than intervals.

STEM aka **BEAM, NOTE BEAM, NOTE STEM**. The vertical line connecting the note head and its flag.

STEP Any single increment between adjoining pitches on a scale. For example, a whole step is two semitones, a half step is one.

STOP Organ lever that opens or closes a pipe or set of pipes. Also, to use the fingers to change the vibrating length of a string, or to place the hand into the bell of a horn.

STRETTO (It.) Usually, a concluding passage performed at an increased tempo; in a **FUGUE**, an overlapping of two statements.

STRINGENDO (It.) Quicken the tempo.

SUBDOMINANT	The fourth degree of the **DIATONIC SCALE**, or a chord with its **TONIC** (root) so located. See Chapters 8, 10, 12.
SUBITO	(It.) "Suddenly," "immediately."
SUBJECT	The basic thematic material of a musical work.
SUITE	A collection of short, contrasting independent pieces; often, a collection of themes extracted from a larger work, such as a **BALLET**.
SUSPENSION	In general, the use within a chord of a tone foreign to its structure which results in making the harmony subjectively ambiguous. e.g., **SUSPENDED FOURTH**: replacing the third in a chord with the fourth. See Chapter 12.
SYMPHONIC POEM	aka **TONE POEM**. A one-movement orchestral work with program notes suggesting a theme or story line. Developed in 19th century Europe.
SYMPHONY	A composition for orchestra, comprising four movements: **ALLEGRO, ADAGIO, SCHERZO,**and **ALLEGRO**.
SYNCOPATION	Placement of rhythmic accents at unexpected points in a pattern, or on weak beats.
SYNTHESIZER	Any electronic instrument capable of generating sound waves in various relationships.

T

TABLAS	A set of tunable North Indian single-headed hand drums, the **TABLA** and the **BAYA**.
TABLATURE	A guitar chord or fingering diagram.
TACET	(Latin) A direction to refrain from playing for an extended period of time, often an entire movement.
TAIKO DRUMS	Ceremonial Japanese drumming ensembles emphasizing spiritual, physical, and musical disciplines.
TAMBOURINE	A small-frame hand drum with metal jangles suspended within the frame.

TAMBORIM	Small Brazilian single-headed frame drum without jangles, played with a single stick. Pitch is altered by varying finger pressure on the head.
TAMBOUR	(Fr.) "Drum."
TAMBURA	The four-string **LUTE** of Persia and India that performs the **DRONE** part in a **RAGA**.
TAM-TAM	Gong, especially in a tuned set in a **GAMELAN** orchestra. Also, the gamelan bells.
TANGO	Argentinean dance developed in Buenos Aires and Montevideo, from a combination of cultural influences, towards the end of the 19th century. A medium-slow couples dance in four-four, featuring posturing and dramatic movement. Main instruments are **FIDDLES** and the **BANDONEON** (accordion).
TARANTELLA	(It.) Italian folk dance in two sections, the second features an **ACCELERANDO** to the finish. Associated with the tarantula, whose poisonous bite the dance was supposed to cure.
TEMPERAMENT	Fine-tuning of an instrument by deviating from acoustically correct intervals, according to a system of dividing the octave; allows for greater flexibility of harmonic progression.
TEMPLE BLOCKS	Hollowed hardwood blocks, sounding various pitches when struck. Arranged in sets.
TEMPO	(It.) Technically, the speed of the music. Determined relatively by terms (e.g., **ALLEGRO**, **LARGO**, etc.), and precisely by **METRONOME MARKING** (e.g., $\quarternote = 120$).
TENOR	The highest-range male vocal part. Range: *Bb* (115 Hz) to *bb'* (460 Hz).
TENOR DRUM	A marching drum, without snares.
TENOR SAXOPHONE	See **SAXOPHONE**.
TENSION	The anticipation of a release or resolution in music. Suggested by rhythm, melody, harmony, dynamics, or a combination of these. Also, the tightness of a string, drum head, or snare.
TENUTO	(It.) See **SOSTENUTO**.

TESSITURA   (It.) Generic term for **RANGE**.

THEME   The melody, subject.

THEME AND VARIATION   Compositional technique of elaboration on a subject by adding subsequent repetitions featuring significant modification of qualities such as **TEMPO, ARTICULATION, RHYTHM**, etc.

THROUGH BASS   See **BASSO CONTINUO**.

THROUGH-COMPOSED   A style of songwriting providing different music for each **STANZA**.

THUMB PIANO   See **KALIMBA**.

TIMBALES   Tunable single-headed drums with metal shells, used in Afro-Cuban and similar music, played with hands and dowel sticks on heads and sides. A cowbell is usually mounted between a pair of these drums.

TIMBRE   (Fr.) Tone, tone color; the identifying tone quality of a voice or instrument, based on the harmonic composition of the sound it produces.

TIMPANI (TYMPANI)   See **KETTLE DRUMS**.

TIN WHISTLE   See **PENNY WHISTLE**.

TOCCATA   (It.) A composition for the keyboard, designed to display the performer's finger dexterity and the resources of the instrument.

TOM-TOM   Generic term for tunable, mid-range drums, pitched above the bass drum.

TONALITY   Refers to the central tone (**KEY**) of a given piece of music; sometimes the term is used to define adherence to key (as opposed to **ATONALITY**).

TONE CLUSTER   A dissonant group of pitches pitched close together, sounded simultaneously.

TONE COLOR   aka **TIMBRE**. The combination of a fundamental and its particular harmonics to produce a characteristic sound, or tone quality. See Chapter 8.

TONE ROW   See **SERIES**.

TONIC The central tone or pitch. The first degree of any scale or key. See Chapters 10, 11.

TONMEISTER (Ger.) A broadcast, sound, or recording engineer with training in musical theory, acoustics, and aesthetics.

TRANSPOSE To write or perform a piece of music in a key other than the original.

TRANSPOSING INSTRUMENTS Any whose fundamental resonating pitch is not *C*, or which are built in keys other than *C*.

TRANSVERSE FLUTE Any flute played from the side rather than end-blown.

TRAPS Common name for all drum kit accessories (e.g., bells, rachets, etc).

TRATTENUTO (It.) Indication to hold back the tempo.

TREBLE CLEF See **G-CLEF**.

TREMOLO (It.) A trembling, quivering tonal effect; A kind of rapid, narrow **VIBRATO**.

TRIAD A chord composed of three tones. See Chapter 12.

TRIANGLE A steel bar bent into a triangular shape and struck with a hammer, stick, or piece of metal, producing complex high frequency combinations and a bell-like sound. Pitch of fundamental varies with length and diameter of bar.

TRILL A melodic ornament consisting of alternating a given note rapidly and smoothly with a neighboring pitch.

TRIO An ensemble of three performers. Also, music written for three parts. Also, the middle section of an **A-B-A COMPOSITION**. See Chapter 7.

TRIPLET A mathematically artificial grouping of three notes of equal value. See Chapter 3.

TRITONE The interval established by moving three whole tones (whole steps) from a given note, i.e., an augmented fourth or diminished fifth. Medieval music composition forbade its use. See **DIABOLUS IN MUSICA**.

TROMBONE	Brass instrument pitched above the **TUBA** and below the **TRUMPET**. A seven-position slide mechanism provides chromatic movement across its range. Some tenor trombones have a valve system. Bass trombones also employ a trigger/rotor to extend lower range. Range: **TENOR TROMBONE:** E (80 Hz) to $c"$ (512 Hz). **BASS TROMBONE:** C (64 Hz) TO bb' (230 Hz).
TROMMEL	(Ger.) Drum.
TROUBADOURS	(Fr.) Poet/musicians in Medieval France and Italy (11th and 12th centuries). Predecessors of the **MINNESINGERS, MEISTERSINGERS,** street poets, and rappers.
TRUMPET	The highest-pitched of the brass instrument family, employing a piston/valve system to achieve a chromatic range from e (160 Hz) to c''' (1,024 Hz) for the standard Bb instrument. The bass trumpet is pitched exactly one octave lower. The C-trumpet, common to **SYMPHONIC** music and **OPERA**, begins its range at $f^{\#}$ (187 Hz). Older music often calls for trumpets in other keys.
TUBA	The lowest-pitched of the brass instruments. The standard orchestra tuba has the same effective range as the **SOUSAPHONE:** FF (44 Hz) to bb (230 Hz). See **WAGNER TUBA.**
TUMBADORA	(Sp.) The largest, lowest pitched **CONGA** drums, of Afro-Cuban origin. The mid-range drum is, technically, the **CONGA;** the highest pitched, the **QUINTO.**
TUMBAO	A basic **CONGA** drum dance beat.
TUBULAR BELLS	See **CHIMES.**
TUNING FORK	A resonating steel fork-shaped device designed to produce a specific pitch when struck; an audio tuning aid.
TUNING SLIDE	A movable section of tubing on a wind instrument permitting an adjustment of length, therefore pitch.
TURN	A melodic ornamentation calling for the addition of supplemental notes to those written. Also the notation symbol for such embellishment. See Chapter 5.
TUTTI	(It.) "All," "everyone." An indication for the entire ensemble to play.

TWELVE-TONE MUSIC   A technique developed by Arnold Schoenberg and others during the 1920's whereby all 12 semitones of the chromatic scale were used sequentially in compositions according to an agreed upon formula. aka **SERIES, TONE ROW, ATONAL MUSIC**.

TZIGANE   (Fr.) Gypsy-style music.

U

UKULELE   The small four-string acoustic guitar adopted by native Hawaiians from the Portuguese during the 18th century. Usually tuned to a C^6 or D^6 chord.

UNA CORDA   (It.) One string. Indication for the use of the piano's soft (left) pedal, permitting the hammer to strike only one string of the tuned sets otherwise activated by the keyboard. Abbr. **U.C.**

UNISON   All voices (instruments) on the same part (melody), or performing the same melody in octaves.

UP BEAT   Generic term for the anticipation before a down beat or cue.

UP BOW   aka **POUSSEZ**. A notation symbol for a string player to start a particular phrase or note on the up stroke. See Chapter 5.

V

VALSE   (Fr.) Waltz. The 18th century European ballroom dance in three-four time.

VAMP   An introductory passage or interlude (often repeated several times) before the melody or a chorus in improvised music; often used in show tunes.

VAUDEVILLE   (Fr.) An outgrowth of 18th century **COMIC OPERA** that evolved into variety stage entertainment in England and the U.S.

VELOCE   (It.) Fast, swiftly.

VERSE   A line (or other group) of lyrics in a popular song, often serving as an introduction.

VIBRAHARP aka **VIBES**. A motorized metal bar **XYLOPHONE** with tubular resonators, invented in the 1920's; revolving metal disks within the resonators create a vibration of the tones produced. Played with two or more mallets.

VIBRA-SLAP A spring-activated percussion instrument that mimics the sound of the **JAW BONE**.

VIBRATO (It.) Any number of vocal and instrumental techniques that produce regular subtle fluctuations of the true pitch, especially on sustained notes. These slight detuning vibrations increase definition of individual voices or parts.

VIGOROSO (It.) Vigorously.

VIOLINS The group of bowed string instruments in the orchestra. The vibrating string principle for producing musical sound is common to most ancient cultures. The modern instruments are as follows:
- **VIOLIN**: g (198 Hz) to g'''' (3,072 Hz)
- **VIOLA**: c (128 Hz) to g''' (1,536 Hz)
- **'CELLO**: C (64 Hz) to g'' (768 Hz)
- **BASS VIOL**: EE (40 Hz) to g' (768 Hz)

VIRGINAL A small version of the **HARPSICHORD**, probably dating from the 15th century. Range: C (64 Hz) to c''' (1,024 Hz).

VIRTUOSO (It.) "Most virtuous." Term of respect referring to a musician of extraordinary skill.

VIVACE (It.) Lively, full of energy.

VOCALESE A style of vocalization using only vowel sounds rather than words; the voice imitating another instrument.

VOICING The act of assigning parts to voices or instruments.

VOLANT (Fr.) At will.

W
....

WAH WAH A type of mute for brass instruments. The name imitates an effect achieved by partially covering, then uncovering, the mute while playing. Also, an electronic pedal control producing a similar effect on the amplified guitar.

WAGNER TUBAS Low range brass instruments built especially for composer Richard Wagner's *Der Ring Des Nibelungen*—"Ring Cycle" of four operas.

WALDHORN (Ger.) The forest horn. A **NATURAL HORN** in the **FRENCH HORN** range. aka **ALPEN HORN**.

WALTZ (Ger.) See **VALSE**.

WASHBOARD Used in cajun, zydeco, and sometimes country music as a percussion instrument: worn strapped to the chest and scraped with finger thimbles.

WOOD BLOCK A piece of carved or slit wood mounted on the bass drum in a **KIT**, and used in place of **CLAVES** or **TEMPLE BLOCKS**.

WOODWINDS The family of wind instruments originally made from wood. Today, all flutes and reeds.

X

XYLOPHONE A percussion instrument comprising tuned wood bars or keys, originating in the far East, brought to India, then Africa, and finally to Europe in the 15th century. The range for the standard instrument is: f' (352 Hz) to c'''' (4,096 Hz). See **MARIMBA**.

Y

YODEL A singing style originating in Switzerland and Austria and employed by folk and country singers, employing the technique of interspersing **FALSETTO** notes throughout melodic material with ease and intonation control. A similar technique exists in some African singing styles.

Z

ZAPATEADO (Sp.) A type of **FLAMENCO** dance in three-four time for a solo performer. A "shoe dance."

ZARZUELA (Sp.) A music drama, usually comic, sometimes involving audience participation.

ZINKE (Ger.) A **CORNETT** formed from an animal's horn, like the **SHOFAR**.

ZITHER (Ger.) A folk instrument common to many cultures, consisting of a sound box (held at the chest) with multiple strings played with both hands, producing both melody and harmony. Various tunings and ranges. Played solo, ensemble, or to accompany vocals.

ZYDECO A blend of Creole and cajun traditional dance music, popular in Louisiana, featuring vocals, accordion, fiddle and drums.

CPSIA information can be obtained
at www.ICGtesting.com
Printed in the USA
FSOW02n0953281217
42394FS